WHY BILLY GRAHAM?

WHY BILLY GRAHAM?

David Poling

ZONDERVAN
PUBLISHING HOUSE   OF THE ZONDERVAN CORPORATION
GRAND RAPIDS, MICHIGAN 49506

Library of Congress Cataloging in Publication Data

Poling, David, 1928-
   Why Billy Graham?

    1. Graham, William Franklin, 1918-   2. Evan-
gelists—United States—Biography.   I. Title.
BV3785.G69P59   269'.2'0924 [B]   77-13195
ISBN 0-310-36350-0

*For Lois Jackson and Carol King,
whose talent in research and typing
made this book happen*

Contents

Preface

This is a book about one of the most widely known and respected Christians in the world — Billy Graham. It is written from the perspective of one who has not always appreciated the methods of mass evangelism nor cherished the techniques of the Graham organization. Indeed, if you would poke through the pages of the *New York Times* and *Saturday Review* in the mid–1960s, you would discover my early complaints of the Graham style of persuading people to become Christians. In the past decade my thinking has changed drastically concerning the ministry of America's most famous Christian and the impact his preaching is now having around the world.

Nowhere is the Christian community better observed than in the public proclamation of the gospel — and never more vulnerable than in the ministry of an evangelist or revivalist. The picture of a shouting, stomping preacher, mouthing old phrases and worn-out words, has been a favorite of the motion picture industry (especially old Westerns) where the image of a clergyman is a frighteningly sub-Christian cartoon.

More than any other person in modern history, Billy Graham has discredited this caricature to reveal an evangelist's role as one of the most respected in our time. This book is my attempt to explain the success of this prominent preacher and how that achievement, after nearly thirty years of public attention, is shaping the lives of millions of people.

I have written this book for two special groups: first, the extensive gathering of Graham's followers, many of them new Christians, who want to know more about the struggles and difficulties in Billy's own growth as a Christian, plus a better understanding of some of the conflicts that have divided Christians into separate, opposing camps. Billy went through a long period of sifting and sorting ideas before he discovered the common ground upon which Christians could unite in presenting God's Word to the world. You will discover the real genius that belongs to Billy: the gift of illustration and example, which so many people take for granted.

Second, I wrote this book for my friends, many of them sharply critical and anxious about the man from North Carolina. Now crowded into silence — or at least heavily sedated by Graham's unbelievable success, stamina, and the new position of Christian statesman — they need a fresh vision. My hope is that the opponents of Billy's mission will come to realize that he does not require of them uniformity of doctrine or absolute acceptance of his biblical interpretation — but rather the capacity to love one another and, in that love, to be a witness to the whole world. To know Billy Graham personally is to know a gentle, graceful, caring spirit — and in that friendship to experience the grace of our Lord Jesus Christ.

I also wrote this book for myself. This project became a long-needed recovery operation of reclaiming and renewing my own evangelical roots which put such a powerful focus on Jesus Christ, a keen interest in the authority of the Scriptures, and a generous view of other Christians beyond one's own denominational loyalty. To be evangelical and ecumenical is to return to the surging stream that expressed so much mission of the early church in Asia Minor and the later church in early America.

G. K. Chesterton once wrote that the world is getting older and older and the Christian church is getting younger and younger. What did he mean but that the vitality and energy of our faith is fresh every morning with new hopes and promises, that Christ personally renews those who give their allegiance to His way. Surely the most significant part of Billy Graham's success is his faith and trust in God. Through the evangelist's mission, Jesus Christ has been lifted up in our time.

DAVID POLING

CHAPTER 1

The World Was Ready

The World Was Ready

After World War II, a major religious reawakening swept across the United States. The surge toward the recovery of family life (delayed for millions by the global conflict) and the desire to settle down after so many years of upset, disarray, and death brought many people to a fresh awareness of their spiritual need. New cars, new homes, new jobs were evident everywhere. Booming colleges and university growth, coupled with aspirations for international understanding, intensified the search for wholeness and spiritual belonging. Churches experienced sudden growth. Church attendance reached a high for the twentieth century. Financial strength flowed into local congregations, and the baby boom crowded Sunday schools with future members of tomorrow's church.

In fact, everything was primed for a great tomorrow. The stock market was building toward a postwar record height. Television began its dazzling entry into the minds of Western civilization, promising information and entertainment on a level never before experienced or enjoyed. Electronics became a code word for a magical future. And Americans added their special seasoning to all this social, political, and economic excitement by moving all over the place, but mostly from East to West, searching for the nicer home, a better job, a happier marriage.

In all this sunshine and song of the early fifties, a dark, ugly, and frightening cloud rose to the ceiling of the human skyline — the hydrogen bomb. Its atmospheric presence, resulting from testing and retesting, reminded Americans and Russians as well as the rest of the world of the stark horror of intercontinental destruction. Atomic warfare was not only possible, but a reality for East–West relationships. The wartime allies who had rid the world of Hitler now seemed capable of doing the same with each other. The Communists' expansion into Eastern Europe—linked with their success in China and the Far East — brought fresh torment, suspicion, and fear to the Americans. The citizens of North America thought they had already invested enough in World War II, now to enjoy peace, international tranquillity, and the satisfaction of postponed personal ambitions. Things were turning sour. Washington politicians were replaying the corruption game. The stock market turned belly up. Cars and homes had a tasteless fulfillment, bringing buckets of indebtedness. And the people in church seemed to be milling around without direction or motivation.

In this climate of frustration and anger and apprehension, Billy Graham began his preaching ministry, and his audience growth was amazing. In September 1949, following the spectacular atomic–hydrogen display of the American–Russian weapons testing (and prior to the anguish of the Korean conflict which verified the Iron Curtain between East and West), Billy Graham arrived in California.

Billy had been pastor of a small congregation in Western Springs, Illinois, in the late forties. Fresh out of Wheaton College, Graham persuaded his hundred-member congregation to sponsor a Sunday evening radio show on a Chicago station. "Songs in the Night" combined the warmth of gospel music, crisp biblical messages by Graham, and a midwestern folksiness that caught on immediately. Shortly after that, George Beverly Shea joined the program as soloist and announcer.

Billy's talent, plus his yearning for a wider outreach, brought him in touch with "Youth for Christ," an organization whose purpose is to evangelize high-school-age youth. He became their principal evangelist for three years, 1946–49. As his experience strengthened his convictions, an evangelistic association was formed in Minneapolis, and the early team started to function professionally and enthusiastically. Youth for Christ gave Billy a firsthand grasp of the spiritual struggle going on in the lives of thousands of young people in Western society; his campaigns not only covered every state in the Union, but also much of Europe and Great Britain. As Youth for Christ began achieving measurable success, the mainline churches promptly greeted this surging growth with derision and putdown: too literal about the Bible, too arrogant toward existing congregations, and too self-righteous toward the historic roots of religion. Much of this controversy came from the clergy who saw their own youth groups stumbling. They resented outsiders, flourishing under new techniques of personal evangelism and — led by bright young leaders such as Graham — communicating a red-hot gospel.

However, the liberal magazine *Christian Century*, establishment father of the mainline Protestant churches, had to admit that something more than a ministerial sneer should greet the success of Youth for Christ.

> Yet the fact that it has gone so far as it has is proof that something close to spiritual famine exists among large sections of our population, including rising generations, who are more hungry for faith than their elders. The churches are not feeding these starving people and they cannot be indifferent to the challenge which this attempt to use new channels of communication for preaching the gospel offers them. They should do likewise and better.[1]

The appearance of Graham in Los Angeles marked the young pastor's breakthrough as a celebrated evangelist and preacher. Not that his Youth for Christ days were unsuccessful or ordinary — he is known to have gained some 7,000 youth converts for Christ in a single year. Yet nothing in his experience, nothing in the early New England rallies, nothing in Chicago or Baltimore would compare to the spiritual explosion that was to be revealed in the Los Angeles meetings that would finally bring the full force of even the secular press behind this young preacher from North Carolina. William Randolph Hearst sent his famous note to his editors after observing the extraordinary influence of this young preacher; two words: "Puff Graham." Hearst may have been the ignition point, but friends of Graham would answer that he had something to puff that belonged neither to the press or grandfather Hearst's conclusion: Graham had the American restlessness and uneasiness by the throat. And he understood the timeless message of Jesus Christ to reach and reclaim these people who honestly sought newness of life, and wholeness in the Spirit of God.

To Billy Graham, more than any other person in the last half of the twentieth century, was given that particular skill of preaching which was accompanied by a special insight into Scripture and human events, an understanding of the inner hunger, the gasping spiritual thirst that afflicted so many millions of inhabitants of Western civilization. I was tempted to say inhabitants of the United States, but Billy's worldwide ministry keeps crowding into my thoughts, and it was there in those Los Angeles days that this witness bloomed with such vigor and influence.

He was soon saying, with that Southern accent that startled some and put off others, some crisp, cutting conclusions about life:

All humanity is seeking the answers to the confusion, the moral sickness, the spiritual emptiness that oppresses the world. All mankind is crying out for guidance, for comfort, for peace. . . . We talk of peace but are confronted by war. We devise elaborate schemes for security but have not found it. We grasp at every passing straw and even as we clutch, it disappears.[2]

The evangelist built his initial preaching around this hungering search, the "Great Quest" as he would later label it in his book, *Peace With God*. At first we thought that political freedom was the saving answer and when the world was politically liberated, happiness would break out. When this failed so utterly, with staggering corruption in all levels of government, no matter if totalitarian or free, men and women chased a new faith in education. And this young tree planted and watered and trusted later revealed the same elements of decay, the same towering disappointments, for as the evangelist concluded about those miles of college graduates,

> Though our heads are crammed with knowledge, our hearts are empty. . . . We are the most informed people in the history of civilization — and yet the most miserable.[3]

Then Billy came to the heartbreak of California (which was really the regret of all America but done in a flashier, most casual style):

> The brightest, most inviting path of all was the one marked higher standards of living. Almost everyone felt he could trust this one to carry him automatically into that better and more joyful world. This was felt to be the sure route. . . . This was the path that led through the beautiful full-color magazine advertisements, past all the shining new cars, past the gleaming rows of electric refrigerators and automatic washing machines, past all the fat chickens cooking in the brand-new copper bottomed pots. We knew we'd hit the jackpot this time . . . but has it made us happy? Has it brought us the joy and satisfaction and the reason for living that we were seeking? No.[4]

Those sermons of the early Graham era were marked with a lethal application that reminds us thirty years later that he has always had the knack of knowing his audience, sensing where they are hurting and hoping, and is prepared to intensify that hurting and hoping before offering the helping, saving message of Christ.

Again, those California nights heard that Southern accent hammering home the truth into so many shallow lives:

> America is said to have the highest per capita boredom of any spot on earth! We know that because we have the greatest variety and greatest number of artificial amusements of any country. People have become so empty that they can't even entertain themselves. They have to pay other people to amuse them, to make them laugh, to try to make them feel warm and happy and comfortable for a few minutes, to try to lose that awful, frightening, hollow feeling . . . that terrible, dreaded feeling of being lost and alone.

Billy spoke steadily of the three facts that "constitute the true story of man:

his past is filled with sin,
> his present is overflowing with sorrow,
>> and the certainty of death faces
>> him in the future."

The answer is Jesus Christ, "the same yesterday, and to-day, and for ever."[5]

Billy had a clarity and freshness that urged his listeners to get up out of their seats and come forward and claim it in a commitment to Christ.

That was the formula. Critics called it manipulative, staged, commercial. Yet faithful people argued, convincingly, that God's Spirit was stirring in Los Angeles. The initial five weeks swelled into a massive sixth week, with not only thousands in attendance, but some 700 of the 1000 Los Angeles congregations now supporting the Graham crusade. Among those who came forward, hesitantly, reluctantly, certainly wonderingly were show-business personalities, professional mobsters, and outstanding sports figures. Graham had become a celebrity, a celebrity for Christ, who like Paul declared that "I am made all things to all men, that I might by all means save some" (1 Cor. 9:22).

By now, in this third decade of Billy Graham's successful ministry, you have heard of the thousands who have come forward and the thousands more, perhaps, who have made their quiet resolution at home to follow Jesus Christ as a result of this evangelist's preaching. What is essential to grasp is the reality that Graham's persuasive preaching has a second- and third-wave effect *through* the lives of those who are converted. And just as important is this: Graham's influence today is founded on the same formula and strategy of almost thirty years ago — an absolute trust in the power of God; a conviction concerning the living spiritual strength of the risen Lord; total trust in the power of prayer; the openness to believe that God will do new and wonderful things through those who love Him and His Word.

It is fair to argue that Graham's preaching themes over the years rarely change, only the illustrations. While it is true that his theological perspective has widened with his experience, it is just as correct to state that his primary topic is the emptiness, loneliness, spiritual vacuum of men and women, their lostness in sin, and sorrow over death. These are as current as next Christmas and unless these needs, hurts, and sorrows are covered by Christ's redeeming love, the situation only turns to despair.

A brilliant example of what we are talking about is illustrated in Charles Colson's book, *Born Again.* This Watergate personality was as tough and cunning as any person in the Nixon administration. His scheming manner and hardness of heart were vocabulary terms for the Washington cocktail circuit, words used by people suspicious and afraid. While Colson feared no one, he was haunted by the inner self, a solitary spiritual torment. During a visit with Tom Phillips, the president of Raytheon Corporation, the dynamics of a religious experience were revealed to Colson by this friend:

> My life wasn't complete, Chuck. I would go to the office each day and do my job, striving all the time to make the company succeed, but there was a big hole in my life. I began to read the Scriptures, looking for answers. Something made me realize I needed a personal relationship with God. One night I was in New York on business and noticed that Billy Graham was having a Crusade in Madison Square Garden. I went — curious, I guess — hoping maybe I'd find some answers. What Graham said that night put it all into place for me. I saw what was missing, the personal relationship with Jesus Christ, the fact that I hadn't ever asked Him into my life, hadn't turned my life over to Him. So I did it — that very night* at the Crusade.[6]

More discussions followed. Bible reading began. Books, such as C. S. Lewis's classic, *Mere Christianity,* became bedside companions for the groping, deeply disturbed Colson. Then on a Friday morning, staring off into the Atlantic Ocean surf, Charles Colson offered these words:

> Lord Jesus, I believe You. I accept You. Please come into my life. I commit it to You.

It is not inaccurate to say that Billy Graham, by his appeal and persuasion through Tom Phillips, reached one of the most notorious figures of the Watergate era with the good news of Christ . . .

---

*June 1969

yet it was ultimately the love of God made clear and new that operated in the personalities of all three.

THE AUDIENCE WIDENS

As Graham gained a wider and more popular acceptance following the Los Angeles Crusade, invitations from other cities arrived. Known for some overseas rallies for Youth for Christ in the late forties, Billy now was sought as a major evangelist by orthodox Christian groups in England and Scotland as well as in Europe. His success began to create the aura of expectation and more success. Part of this growth period can be credited probably to the vast outreach of his publication, *Decision,* as well as the popular radio program heard nationwide, "Hour of Decision." By 1955, this evangelistic Sunday program was broadcast on 700 stations in North America, and the audience was estimated to be in excess of 20 million.

Billy's books were enjoying a phenomenal sale. *Peace With God,* a volume of some eighteen sermons, read as well as his original delivery of the sermons. More than 500,000 copies were in print by the mid-fifties. Much of this early success should be traced to the open, innovative personality of Graham and the encouragement by his team. They were men and women who were consumed by a zeal for preaching the gospel to the whole world. Their Southern Baptist connections did not hurt, for they were a group of Christians who were tirelessly extending the lines and faith of the Christian life in urban areas all over America; they were hardly confined to the boundaries of the Mason-Dixon line. Much of what they said and did irritated conservative Presbyterian/Episcopalian types. They seemed so flashy in dress, so with-it in style. They moved in radio and television circles with such ease, with an instant willingness to experiment. They were certainly daring with the dollars. Mainline Christians, at least among the clergy, were shocked by their sudden success, for they were working in urban areas that long since appeared to have said good-by to Christianity or at least to the interpretation favored by historic old churches. The Graham Team moved into the secular city with both hands, using billboards and bumper stickers and musical stars and flashing lights and a professional knack that strengthened whatever they were doing — all in the name of Christ. Deep down they were resented by the establishment churches of the land. They had become so popular, so obviously successful that the only answer to their success was that they must be advocating a shallow Christianity, a temporary faith, a sort of football tournament of religion, meeting in public arenas and outdoor stadiums.

The Graham thrust was hitting the old churches where it hurt: evangelism. They nailed thousands of back-sliding Christians with a fresh, personal gospel. The ivy-league critics were certain that this was really revivalism, not evangelism, and it took long definitions and panel discussions for interested Christians to sort out those differences, which rarely mattered to the man in the street.

The unmentioned topic of the fifties and sixties (regarding Billy's success and his torrid pace of achievement and influence) was simply professional jealousy. Clergy often are apprehensive about churchmen who surface as an unusual personality within the life of the larger society. Names such as Peale, Sheen, and Graham became amazingly popular in North America for several decades. I know, for I shared hostility toward them and expressed it in refined, acceptable ways. So did my colleagues in the ministry. This is not to set aside the legitimate concerns that gracious and thoughtful people have expressed about the Graham revivals or the Peale promotions of the early fifties. There is always the necessity and, it is hoped, always the room for sound differences in the life of the Christian family. When they carefully and thoughtfully emerge, it reveals an inner strength of the body of Christ to correct some excesses or lift up some neglected areas of the gospel. But the critics of Graham — largely the seminaries and certain leading pastors of the Eastern seaboard — went after the preacher from North Carolina as if he were Lucifer himself.

Some of the doubters showed restraint and Christian reserve in their complaints. Frequently these topics were aired in scholarly journals, especially the liberal *Christian Century*, which published a searching piece by Reinhold Niebuhr who was, in 1956, the crown prince of the reigning neoorthodox establishment of Protestant Christianity.

> I have no business making any proposals to Billy Graham. We are not acquainted. But I share general approval of his modesty and sincerity in the Christian community and also a certain uneasiness that his type of evangelism may seem to be irrelevant to the great moral issues of our day.[7]

Niebuhr's proposal to Graham was that he take a more aggressive stance against the evils of segregation and link his call for the sinner's repentance with a willingness to regard racial prejudice as a primary block to one's salvation. During this era the whole civil rights protest movement was under way. Martin Luther King, Jr., was embarked on his nonviolent crusade for justice. Congress was locked in the intensity of debates over new laws to reflect the rights of the black community for equal housing, education, and employment. The Public Accommodations Act was soon to be debated. Churchmen close to Niebuhr were bearing abuse, shock, and at times, death for putting their faith on the line. Many felt that Billy was distantly supporting them, but was too vague or impersonal in his application of salvation for the ills of society as well as the individual believer. Was religion social or personal?

Dr. Niebuhr quoted a Jewish friend who had witnessed one of Billy Graham's revivals in the city of Richmond, Virginia, and who had made some pertinent remarks about the nature of the revival. "We Jews," he wrote, "are naturally critical not only because such a revival, with its emphasis upon a commitment in religious terms to which Jews cannot subscribe, tends to widen the chasm between Jews and Christians, which common devotion to civic decencies has tended to bridge, but also because the commitment does not include a new attitude on the race issue, which is so desperately needed today."[8]

Niebuhr expressed doubt that the Graham Crusades could accomplish much:

> Revivalistic Christianity has not been particularly effective in challenging collective evil. It grew to power on the frontier, where

its moral appeals were limited to the condemnation of drunkenness, adultery, and sabbath violations. It may not be entirely unfair to observe that the section of the country in which the present crises in race relations is most acute is precisely that section which has experienced annual revivals, all calculated to redeem the sinner and guarantee the perfection of a truly "committed" soul.[9]

Alas, the judgment of time is ruthless on even the most brilliant and thoughtful Christians. Boston, the heartland of New England liberalism and the mecca of Civil War righteousness for the Lord, has become in these latter days just as vindictive and mean on the race question as any city suggested in the South by Dr. Niebuhr twenty years ago.

The so-called "revivals," put down by the establishment churches and held in such suspicion by Niebuhr, were the source of inspiration for a southern governor, Jimmy Carter, who brought major advances for black people in Georgia (with a picture of Martin Luther King, Jr., in his executive office) and who today freely "praises the Lord" for his conversion to Jesus Christ. It might be asked, before we are finished with this discussion, what the progressive branch of the Christian community has to offer in place of the challenge, excitement, and personal commitment of a Graham Crusade. Niebuhr spoke of the southern piety as being "a quaint vestige." Revivals too often generated a "widespread naive enthusiasm" — yet it is our opinion that history will vindicate the Graham Crusades; that piety is not to be erased from the Christian life; that enthusiasm is what the world, much less the Church, needs to have in order to accomplish anything worthwhile.[10]

FROM EUROPE TO AMERICA

While criticism continued to mount concerning Graham's success and advance in North America in this period, his schedule included a heavy series of meetings in Great Britain and Europe. The Christian and secular response to this American evangelist generated lively discussions in the London *Times* and spirited interviews on radio and television. One Anglican canon observed regretfully,

The recent increase of fundamentalism among university students cannot but cause concern. Universities exist for the advancement of learning. On that basis, therefore, can fundamentalism claim a hearing at Cambridge?[11]

Yet Billy took on combative Cambridge as well as sophisticated London. A correspondent for *Time* magazine recalled his 1955 university appearance:

He stood in the cramped quarters of the pulpit before a crowd of 1,200 which had left behind an overflow queue two blocks long. When he began to speak, probably no more than 10 percent of them were wholeheartedly for him.

But Billy's face never lost its smile. Admitting that he found the pulpit confining, he told about the little girl who watched a preacher ranting and jumping about in the pulpit and asked her mother, "What will we do, Mother, if he gets out?"

. . . He said over and over again, "This is what the Bible says. . . ."

One exasperated young intellectual exclaimed aloud (on the second night), "Really, you can't get away with that, Billy!"

But the students continued to come and stayed silent and impressed. Once when a divinity professor introduced him with the reminder he could not agree with his doctrinal views, Billy rose in the tense silence and said that he did not think that kind of disagreement made much difference. "We are all Christians and we love one another," he said. "A minister is not a minister unless he is winning men to Christ. If theological students don't think they can do that, they should quit studying for the ministry." The students applauded for three minutes.[12]

We ought to be clear about the rash of invitations to conduct Crusades in Europe. The Christian community is a state church in Germany, England, or Scotland as well as the free church anywhere in the British Isles (known as "evangelicals" in France, Holland, and Italy). All were steadily being squeezed, ignored, and finally squashed by the mature secularism of Western society. Catholics and Protestants were a dwindling group. Religion in Great Britain was something observed under glass in a dusty museum. The champions of the Christian cause were almost invisible. So the appearance of Billy Graham on British soil brought some glimmer of hope and excitement to Christian churches who had not sustained their membership nor seen new faces for generations.

Graham's arrival in England, however, could not have been on a lower note. An advance publication distributed by the Crusade organization had this unfortunate quotation from the evangelist:

> When the War ended (World War II), a sense of frustration and disillusionment gripped England; and what Hitler's bombs could not do, socialism with its accompanying evils shortly accomplished. England's historic faith faltered. The churches still standing were gradually emptied.[13]

The fury of the British Labor Party is hard to imagine, for its leaders had just completed the grand design of a comprehensive socialist government. Graham wired his apologies from aboard ship in the middle of the Atlantic. Associate George Wilson acknowledged that the word "socialism" should have read "secularism," but the proofreaders failed to catch this in the Minneapolis printshop. Whatever, Graham got the ball behind his own goal line and the British press seemed eager to keep him from scoring anywhere on the field.

When the Crusade began in London, England's largest paper, *The Daily Mirror*, with nearly five million readers, noted that

> The overpresentable young man from North Carolina took on the Devil in this sporting palace where dog racing was in full flight less than a hundred yards away. I must say, it was a thundering good contest.[14]

The British mocking humor, seasoned with its righteous, secular stance toward *anything* spiritual or faintly religious, found fulfillment in the columns of *The Daily Express*:

> Former chief correspondent Rene MacColl: "Billy is only one of that great American type — the clean-cut, fast talking, well-groomed Salesman."
>
> Industrial writer: "Efficiency in everything — even to marshaling 300 penitents."
>
> Woman columnist: "I have experienced this sort of thing before . . . when, for instance, I watch Mr. Frankie Laine. . . ."
>
> Literary critic: "'It has been a long time,' thundered Billy, 'since the Word of God has been front-page news.' The words fell like wet pennies into a pool of mud, before a faint titter went round

at the expense of the Press."
Theater critic: "Snappy suit, an eager beak of a nose. The regular-
guy face of an American toothpaste advertisement. . . . He
spoke of divine torments with no suffering in his face . . . of the
Throne of God with no mystery in his voice."[15]

Yet this avalanche of criticism which cascaded on the opening of
the London Crusade was to yield to one of the great revivals in
British history. Day after day the impact of Billy's message and
the winsomeness of his warm personality gathered an enormous
attendance for the evening meetings. Concluded the *London
Daily Telegraph:*

When Mr. Billy Graham's visit to this country was announced, it
was widely feared that he was another American hot gospeler after
the manner of Aimee McPherson (of Four Square Gospel Fame,
Los Angeles). . . . Such impressions were quickly dispelled by his
charm, sincerity, and simplicity bound together by a deep Christian charity.[16]

Not only was Billy responsible for 10,000 decisions for Christ, but
everywhere church attendance began to climb. Not only was the
evangelist heard by the thousands who jammed Harringay Arena,
but also "he invades the London pubs for heart-to-heart talks with
their habitues (he orders lemonade)."[17] In the final days of the
Crusade, the Archbishop of Canterbury, Dr. Geoffrey Fisher,
marveled that "opposition to your crusade has virtually disap-
peared."

One correspondent for an American journal suggested the
secret to Graham's triumph (which Billy would swiftly correct and
say, "Christ's victory!") in the cool, rainy British Isles was that

in London as in America, Billy Graham is revealing himself as
extraordinarily teachable and humble, considering that he is surrounded with the fevered adulation of crowds so much of the time.
He will learn a great deal in London and will, if he keeps up the
growth which has characterized his last three years, put what he
learns to good use for Christ and the church.[18]

The puzzling thing about Graham is that often in his preaching he
reflects such a fiery, unyielding, authoritarian personality — a
determination linked with an underlay of anger or wrath keeps
pushing out to the audience, demanding acceptance and deci-

sion. A sense of dread and alarm can rise out of his pulpit style. Yet his followers would reply that this is essential when you care for wretched lives that must be snatched back from depravity and sin: their condition when they are apart from God. Privately, the evangelist is a warm, laughing, and caring gentleman. He is natural in friendship and open to new ideas and new understandings. Over the years this cordiality has increased and his sternness softened, but not the urgency to preach with large conviction to the lost or sliding.

CHAPTER 2

The Price of
Immediate Success

CHAPTER 2

The Price of
Immediate Success

We often speak of the successes of the Graham Crusades, his triumphs in Britain, or his incredible achievements in this city or that university. What we may be momentarily forgetting is the readiness of the individual, the haunting search for spiritual food, the desperate lunge for release from old sins or broken patterns of ethical behavior. Everyone wants life; many want a new life. Graham's arrival frequently sparks a man or woman with a fresh urgency to do something about an old problem or an unresolved conflict. Our secular world is seething with millions of people in such a condition. And of the millions, many are young people. Why do they respond with such excitement and zeal for the message of the evangelist? Said Billy,

> A youthful mind wants something hard and challenging. When Christianity is made hard and challenging, they will accept it. When you beat around the bush and talk in platitudes, he's not interested. That's the reason communism has the appeal that it does — it offers death. It doesn't offer life. Let's go and die for communism! That appeals to the heroic in a fellow. But Jesus talked about a Cross, too. He said he was on his way to die, but we've been talking about the easy-chair sort of life and never

changing your way of living. Well, when you talk about changing a way of living and living a dedicated life for Christ, taking up the Cross — this will appeal to youth.[1]

The stunning success of the British campaigns of the mid-fifties revealed Billy's understanding of the power of mass communication. Television fed much of Graham's outreach into the English countryside. Public relations techniques were unleashed in a most professional manner, attracting countless thousands to the meetings; yet they also attracted sharp criticism from those who felt differently about the whole enterprise. Such a critic was a Scottish writer, R. B. Robertson, who became infuriated over the "Billy Graham All Scotland Crusade" and wrote a long, scornful article for *Atlantic Monthly* as well as an entire chapter in *Of Sheep and Men* decrying the Crusades publicity in his Scottish, sheepherding town:

> In every well-conducted Scottish parish, never mind one as old and conservative as ours, there is a proper place for putting notices, and that is in the window of the village post office and general store. If we want to know the date of the Lanark Lambing Sales, or which band is playing at the village dance on Saturday night, or who has got a good collie pup for sale, we seek our information in the place where every proclamation of importance to our parish has been made since John Knox announced the Reformation, and maybe long before, back to the news that Graham had breached the Roman Dyke . . . in Mr. Mackay's little window above the postbox.
>
> But this notice wasn't put there. And Mr. Mackay swears he was never asked to put it there, adding as confirmation of his sworn statement that he'd "have torn the bluidy thing up" if he had been asked.
>
> This Graham notice appeared, of all places, at the crossroads!
>
> We have only one crossroads in our parish, where one road leads to the post office, one to the House of Sin, and the third to the Kirk. There is an ancient wooded post at this crossroads which, for differing reasons, we all know well. It is by this post that the daily bus, our only link with urban Scotland, stops for two minutes at 11.54 A.M., it is by this post that the young apprentice-shepherds dawdle of an evening, hoping to waylay Flossie, Tam's teen-age daughter, as she bicycles home down the side road; and it is beside this post that eggs, milk, tatties, newspapers, gardening-tools, sheep-dip powder, and all the commodities that people of a

friendly parish borrow and barter among themselves are left to be picked up. The post is known to some of us for different reasons. It is, as we had discovered, the strategic point where Wee Ecky is usually stationed to keep watch for the policeman or the water bailiff while the Chief Sinner, assisted by the usual few selected law-abiding citizens, is engaged in night operations with flashlights and sharp instruments in the salmon pool below the bridge; and the post is well known, both to car drivers and to those unsteadily on foot, as the major hazard lying between the House of Sin at closing time and the safety of the glens.

Just as the spire of our village Kirk has been, for many centuries, our totem-pole of respectability and our spiritual phallus, so the post by the crossroads has been the symbol and rallying point for all worldly things, including sin. For all we know, it may have stood there since Roman times. It probably has. But, untill Billy Graham came along, nobody ever thought of affixing a notice to it.

We are quite sure Billy Graham put the notice there himself. We do not quite believe the story, which probably originated in the bar of the House of Sin, of a gleaming Cadillac drawing up at the crossroads and a tall handsome young man with nice teeth and hair like the advertisements leaping out and furtively nailing a picture of himself to our post; but we do believe that if, as it is said, Billy Graham is the genius behind his own organization, then it was he and nobody else who decided to put his posters in Scotland anywhere except in the post-office windows, thus getting everybody, in our parish at least, talking about him the very next morning.[2]

Whenever a Christian group approaches the arena of public relations, advertising, and mass communication of the gospel, it faces new perils and opportunities. There is danger of being the huckster, the big-time promoter, the hard-selling salesman which the Christian faith detests and its true believers despise. Yet the advent of printing brought the opportunities of reaching far beyond the sound of a voice. Today the communications miracle is not only global but interterrestrial. Not to take these created gifts from God revealed in the ingenuity of man would be less than Christian — to abuse them or indecently employ them is our worry. Graham became the preeminent representative of the Christian world community by coupling his natural preaching skills to the arrival of these exotic forms and means of communication. The million-circulation tabloids of Great Britain (much,

much larger than anything printed in North America), the vast
network of radio and television broadcasts, the billboards, the
streamers on buses, and yes, the posters on a Scottish "post," all
combined to reveal a Christian dynamic, a gospel appeal to a
society saturated by secular ambitions and sub-Christian ethics,
or even post-Christian morality.

In the closing hours of the London Crusade, one reporter filed
this story to an American audience:

> Billy Graham's Greater London Crusade became an all-England
> crusade. A large cross section of our people have been to Harrin-
> gay Arena where on only four nights has there been an empty seat;
> a hall seating 25,000 could have been filled. Titled nobility, mem-
> bers of Parliament, business men, factory and shop workers have
> felt the impact of the campaign. A number of alcoholics are re-
> ported converted and now attending church.[3]

Most telling in his summary of the Graham impact on British
society, Cecil Northcutt gives us a flashback to the Cambridge
campus where Billy was faulted for his "fundamentalist irrespon-
sibility":

> Perhaps the most remarkable story of the campaign concerns
> Graham's visit to Cambridge to address the undergraduates in the
> university (he spoke separately to student Christian groups as well
> as ministerial candidates).
>
>   At the end of the address he left the hall after asking those who
> wished to make a decision for Christ to remain. He returned 15
> minutes later and found the audience still there. He explained
> again that only those who wished to make a decision should stay.
> Three times he returned thinking there was a mistake. Finally, he
> realized that the young men and women in the hall had decided to
> stay. Then he asked them to come forward, and all rose spontane-
> ously, to make their decision. Truly, a surprising occurrence for
> Cambridge.[4]

If we would assess the reasons for Graham's success in that
sophisticated university town of Old England, in the midst of all
those centuries-filled educational refinement and wealth and
culture called Cambridge, we might dare to say that it was God's
power working through one of His servants. Is that so hard to
believe? Is it just possible that men and women, worn out by the

false promises and deceptive fulfillment of worldly pursuit, would eagerly come forward to make a decision for Christ? Thousands appear to have made that journey of the heart, whether in Cambridge, England, or the Cotton Bowl in Dallas.

Mack Morriss, a Tennessee newspaper editor, said that in his homeland of the South the little people said Billy "has the power." In that countryside filled with ancient Christian folkways preserved in songs and chants, familiar with itinerant healers and not shocked when someone speaks in tongues, these same courthouse whittlers say that ole Billy sure has the power.

Morriss observed the Cotton Bowl appeal when 2,000 came forward:

> They came stunned, weeping, abject, coldly dry-eyed, but rarely, almost never, jubilant. . . . An audience before Billy Graham is a living thing, absorbingly human and interacting. This is why people say he has the power; they can feel him.[5]

What is surprising and convincing about this report is the source. Morriss was not writing for the *Sunday School Times* or the *Christian Herald;* he was reviewing *Peace with God* in the *Saturday Review of Literature!* Familiar with the scientific, educational aura of his readership, Morriss outlined an alternative which he apparently believed personally and urgently enough to lay on his erudite audience:

> This human mass reaction, which has a power all its own, is necessarily missing in Graham's book. But not much else of his evangelism is. It is Billy Graham at full speed, crouched before a microphone, his lean face bright and his long fingers clutched, spilling out an unyielding denunciation of materialism and crying as a voice in the chrome-plated wilderness for repentance, a literal acceptance of Jesus Christ, a literal new birth. When a man becomes a Child of God, Graham preaches from his Bible, he finds the only peace there is, ever, anywhere, with anybody.
>
> Man's conscience or his assent that the morality of the Bible makes sense is not enough. Christ Himself is the answer, not His Sermon on the Mount. Man alone is helpless before a real and resourceful Satan — "a creature of vastly superior intelligence" — and the sins of the world can be atoned only by the blood of Jesus on the cross. Man either believes this or he is lost. Believing it he achieves not only a Heaven "as real as Los Angeles" but a pattern

of living on earth that is a joy itself, because true faith produces obedience and obedience the ability through God's grace to defeat the powers of individual and national darkness.

It can be believed, Billy insists, and, as sin-possessed fingers grip thermonuclear triggers, it must be believed.

Down where I live we've changed a lot since the Scopes trial. Thirty years and TVA and Oak Ridge have seen to that. But even if we haven't we can't be much different now from most Americans — if most Americans are too well-educated to be superstitious, yet too practical to trust our education and too scared to live alone. This is why we don't have many critics of Billy Graham. We would as soon believe Billy's Bible as the physicist who predicts that a cobalt bomb can destroy life as we know it on earth. In fact, many of us would rather.[6]

A subtle change was taking place. The resistance of the secular press was shifting: Graham, if not winning converts among the *Life* and *Look* and *New Yorker* crowd, was certainly gaining appreciation. Nevertheless, the resistance and hostility did not vanish; rather it became more pronounced in the liberal Christian magazine pages (while softening in other journals). The *New Yorker*, long adept at mocking religion and professionally skilled in its caricatures of anything related to the Church, devoted a long and sympathetic report to Graham's appearance in Paris. (He arrived during the height of French fascination with a notorious scandal affecting the Roman Catholic Church, the Vatican, and one Roger Peyrefitte.)

Following Billy's address to some 10,000 people at the Velodrome d'Hiver, the prestigious *Le Monde* was cited by the *New Yorker* and reprinted:

> Is not the availability of such crowds symptomatic in itself? It would be unjust and unpleasant for us to indulge in irony on the American style of such religious manifestation . . . better bow before the spiritual dynamism of this man, whose formula and phrases are perhaps infantile but who touches his public. . . . His technique may offend European intellectuals, but the fact remains that he is successful. The French Protestants who, despite some reservations, did not hesitate to ask him to come to our country made no mistake.[7]

There is no doubt that the London crusades of the mid-fifties were the proving ground for Billy's style of mass evangelism. The additional tours to Scotland and the Continent only provided further assurance, at least to the team of evangelists out of Minneapolis, that they had discovered a winning combination: the great arena or stadium crowd supported by extensive (and expensive) budgets for television and press coverage. Britain was the proving ground, remembered as the cornerstone of Graham's later success in the United States. Risk and daring faith, those qualities (coupled with his own personal, spiritual preparation) were first tried in Los Angeles. But London was the clincher that Billy had a global ministry.

EARLY SUCCESS

Within four years of his emergence as a national religious figure, the secular press was appraising Billy's position, wondering about his income, and predicting a long or short appearance in public life. Since there had never been an evangelist with his perspective and style, critics kept reaching back into American history to find a comparable model. The last significant revivalist was Billy Sunday (a former baseball star) and the two names were certainly similar. The West Coast beginnings of Graham's Crusades also conjured up the California radiance and decline of Aimee Semple McPherson. (Her showmanship, her mysterious private life, and her handle on large resources made for headline copy but only vague consideration by Christian intellectuals or serious scholarly encounter. Reinhold Niebuhr and Ted Gill never addressed questions of concern to Aimee and her following.)

When *Look* identified Billy as the "Barrymore of the pulpit," at thirty-five years of age, the general response of the news magazines and the metropolitan tabloids was to picture the evangelist as a brilliant, even astonishing performer with no accurate grasp of what his faith was all about or how to measure his staying power in the turbulence of public life. He was considered more of a performer, a religious entertainer almost, for as the writers downtown remarked, "he sure can put on a good show." One reporter summed it up for Mr. Mass Media or Miss Madison Avenue by stating,

He's a trouper just as John Barrymore was a trouper and, like Barrymore, there's more than a little ham in him. Like Barrymore, he knows what a handsome profile is worth, and like any other showman, Billy Graham the evangelist, is in business to make a living.[8]

And it was a good living — the best hotel rooms, frequent invitations to use corporate or private planes, and later jets. His books generated a handsome cash flow (which went into trust funds for his children). Newspaper columns and articles for *Reader's Digest* produced a generous yield for winter vacations or a new wing on the residence at Montreat. In his study of Billy Graham, Stanley High recognized the cash criticism that accompanied the early Crusades:

> Earlier in his revival ministry Billy Graham followed the somewhat loose financial practices which have characterized other evangelists and which unhappily in many places seemed to put the dollar sign on revivalists and their methods. Billy Graham's awareness of this problem came to a focus at the end of the six-week crusade in Atlanta, Georgia in 1950. In that Crusade a collection — customarily called a "love offering" — was taken for him and Cliff Barrows. That this method of finance could prove to be a detriment to his ministry was made more apparent by the fact that an Atlanta newspaper published a picture of Billy Graham holding a huge bag which contained this cash collection.[9]

High notes that shortly after this, Billy worked out a plan that completely eliminated the "love offering" and regularized their collections and gifts into a responsible accounting to the public. Billy continued to have a solid income, but holding the money bag would not be his style as once pictured in Atlanta.

Two alarms have always sounded around flashy, religious, public celebrity types: money and women. One of the reasons for the enduring success of Dr. Billy Graham has been his forthright dealing with finance and the public accounting of every Crusade. All the motivations and drives and ambitions of any successful person face the peril of misuse and the distraction of ego needs and basic desires of self. Billy's integration of personality has been on public display for thirty years. He not only preaches the Christian life, but also lives it happily and joyously. He not only survives the perils of "famous men," but gives the world an example of what the Christian commitment in money and power is all about.

The first accountings of the early Crusades show a heavy but not excessive investment in the salaries and expenses of Billy and his team. The Greater Seattle Gospel Crusade of the summer of 1951 was carefully scrutinized by Arthur Lester Frederick for *The Christian Century*. This account not only covered the impact of that interdenominational effort but also gave an analysis of the funds expended:[10]

This study would be incomplete without a statement of the campaign's finances. According to the published report the total amount collected was $190,920.36. Disbursements were as follows:

Advertising, printing and radio	$ 33,080.77
Accommodations, such as rental, equipment, maintenance of stadium	31,160.52
Administration, special services, personal work, follow-ups, etc.	12,396.36
Office expense, stenographers	10,752.41
To cooperating organizations	8,315.00
Salaries to team of four, expense and travel	12,412.51
Love offering for Graham and team and various missionary causes	23,761.58
Graham TV broadcast	30,819.78
"Hour of Decision" broadcast	12,687.31
Miscellaneous	12,548.38
Balance on hand	2,985.74
Total	$190,920.36

Of the almost $191,000 contributed, nearly $124,000 was spent in the Seattle community. The remaining $67,268.67 went to support the "Hour of Decision" broadcast and some other missionary causes approved by the sponsoring churches.

Within the grand total of nearly $200,000 the auditors reported that Billy and his three-person team received salary, expenses, and travel (for forty-two days) of $12,412. That works out to $75 a day per person, which seems rather light under even the most stringent standards. By the time Stanley High was auditing the Nashville Crusade of 1954, the finance committee had already published an accounting in the local newspaper with costs and income spread out over nearly eighty carefully listed items.

Graham's income has been a fascination for the public, or at least for those who inform the public. In the year of the Nashville Crusade, *Newsweek* reported that Billy no longer received *any* income directly from the public meetings. They noted that his annual salary was $15,000, primarily underwritten by interested businessmen. That salary was not out of line for a pastor of a large urban congregation or the head of a Christian college or seminary. Yet the salary fascination continues because of the millions of dollars given in the Crusades. In the mid-sixties, *Christian Herald* coaxed an old team member, Jerry Bevan, to tell all in an article assigned by its then publisher-editor, Ford Stewart. Ford had developed a series of sensational stories about Christian leaders. As he put it, he wanted to know what "kind of guy Graham is in private, I mean, how much does he pay for his suits, what is his annual income, how does he treat people in the back office?" As an associate editor at that time, I recall that Ford was slightly dismayed that from all this research nothing more shocking than a Graham practical joke came to light: getting a staffer to take a mustard tablet instead of an aspirin for an upset stomach! (John Pollock generously assigns this to Ruth Graham.)[11]

As Billy's popularity and, to some, notoriety, increased, so did the volume and intensity of his critics. For some the appearance of Graham in a flashy sport coat or tailored suit (not ever found in a long, black robe complete with collar and tabs, surely) was an insult to the tradition of other days. Donald Meyer of UCLA, writing in *The New Republic*, saves his disgust for the differences he saw in Graham, say, compared with William Jennings Bryan or Billy Sunday or Elmer Gantry:

> Graham is glamorous. Beautifully groomed, beautifully assured, brilliant in profile, beautifully tonic, Graham comes to his audiences, a man who is equipped to meet all the requirements of the American cult of happy, healthy living, popularity and self-assurance.[12]

One is reminded of what Somerset Maugham said in his defense of Kipling. The barrage against the British author followed him long after his death. Max Beerbohm, the American literary critic and book reviewer for countless journals, carried what was once referred to as a "thirty-year war against Rudyard Kipling." Confessed Beerbohm in an interview:

> When I first met him, in Baltimore, he received me so nicely. He was charming. And later . . . so sympathetic, so kind. And then, you know, his books kept coming out, and occasionally I was asked to review them. I couldn't abide them, you know. He was a genius, a very great genius, and I felt he was debasing his genius by what he wrote. . . . You know, I couldn't stop. As his publication increased, so did my derogation. He didn't stop — I couldn't stop. I meant to, I wanted to, but I couldn't.[13]

Of course Maugham, who chose to defend Kipling, suggests some points which may well apply to Graham's career:

> Of course, Kipling had his detractors. The plodding writers who after years of labour had achieved but a modest place in the literary world found it hard to bear that this young man, coming from nowhere, without any of the social graces, should win, apparently with little effort, so spectacular a success; and as we know, they consoled themselves by prophesying (as once before they had of Dickens) that as he had come up like a rocket, he would go down like the stick.[14]

GRAHAM AND HIS CRITICS

Every famous living person attracts a crowd and, for Graham, it was frequently a crowd of critics. His startling success and meteoric rise brought just as swift a response in the writings of those who could not accept his revivalism nor admit that his success could last. The claims of the Graham Team for converts were at times so exuberant (56,000 decisions for Christ in the Madison Square Garden Crusade of 1958) that secular critics arrived to sneer at the statistics and to mock Graham's future success anywhere. Carey McWilliams wrote in *The Nation:*

> On the whole Graham's crusade in New York is about as convincing a demonstration of real religious vitality as the highly pub-

licized American sputnik was a demonstration of American mastery of outer space. Let a few more cold facts about the aftereffects of a Graham crusade break the charm and another episode in American revivalism will be history.[15]

First of all, he was terribly young, especially for a profession called clergy that expected a decent waiting period, say twenty years, before one started receiving awards or gaining on the prizes. Billy seemed to some to be downright unreal. The religious community had not seen the likes of such a personality — perhaps the world was ready, with its custom of child prodigies in music or superstars in sports at the tender age of twenty or younger.

But there were similarities to his presence in history. Remember Frederick Leighton?

At the fresh age of twenty-five, Leighton's *Cimabue's Madonna* was shown at the Royal Academy in London — and promptly purchased by Queen Victoria. Frederick Leighton's career was thus launched by that singular art event in 1855; he went on, to the amazement of his critics and the envy of his peers, to become a major painter in the nineteenth century, spilling over into the entire field of British society as well as arts. His success and following were such that Henry James would write resentfully and enviously,

> his sumptuosity, his personal beauty, his
> universal attainments,
> his portraits of duchesses, his universal
> parties,
> his perfect French and Italian . . . and German,
> his general air of being above all human
> dangers and difficulties![16]

It was too much for one life, even too good to be true, yet there he was, with the art world and the social empire of Victoria at his feet. He was the first artist to be made a peer (Lord) and gracefully used that as a springboard to become President of the Royal Academy, an office and honor he held for twenty years.

The Christian Century, representative of mainline disdain and Eastern suspicion of the Graham galaxy, came at the evangelist with both overseas and domestic critics. One *Century* editor wrote:

By the time these words are read, the Billy Graham crusade will be generating its own kind of excitement and tabulating its own kind of success in New York City. As was arranged long, long ago, Madison Square Garden will be full every night for weeks (maybe months?). The most efficient team of galvanizers on this side of the world will be whipping up nightly enthusiasm by their much-practiced, well-rehearsed methods. Strategists posted around the hall will be waving their hand signals down to the platform suggesting by symbol which of the evangelist's several categorized approaches will work best on a particular pocket of people. The evangelist's forceful press agents will be spreading their own gleaming mathematics over the splendid spectacle. Radio and television will be carrying the voice and image of blond sincerity into homes long conditioned to recognize packaged virtue and desperate now for almost any kind of sincerity. Because news is news, the campaign will be splashed across full columns and the whole pages of newspapers and magazines as long as the furor holds.

It simply cannot fail. The Billy Graham campaign will spin along to its own kind of triumph because canny, experienced engineers of human decision have laid the tracks, contracted for the passengers, and will now direct the traffic which arrives on schedule. The figure is not a remote one. With trainloads of well saved out-of-town supporters coming from as far away as Texas, the campaign will obviously be railroaded to success.[17]

CHAPTER 3

Reaching Out

CHAPTER 3

Reaching Out

Billy Graham's sense of destiny and sense of self are strong and assured. His manner, style, speech, conversation, and warmth have a grace and friendliness that come from the inside. He is at home with movie stars and elderly ladies, talking easily and cordially with waitresses and heads of state. His lanky frame, athletic gait, piercing glance at single faces in the crowd make you realize that he is always reaching out, always available, constantly open to the needs and interests of others. Graham is the number one evangelist in the world today because he never forgets that he is working for Someone else.

This is difficult for professionals in the theater, in films, and in the communications industry to understand. It is particularly true of the press. Graham is powerful in his preaching, but he also is surrounded by a savvy organization of pros who make all the right moves, create the best backup for Crusades, have a canny sense of timing of where Billy should appear and who should make up the host committee in a hundred different cities. They see the big picture and the tiny details. Advance leadership may hit a major urban area a year ahead of the actual Crusade, which might run just seven nights.

In almost every Crusade I have observed, the local press and communications people in radio and television seemed super-hardened and arrogantly braced to deal with this huckster, this latter-day Elmer Gantry, this Billy Sunday with alligator shoes and a lapel mike. They cultivated the old, angry questions of why a Christian needed to invest in tailored suits and trips on private jet planes and be surrounded by a multimillion dollar corporation — especially, they said, when the people who came forward and made a quick emotional decision always fell back to their old hypocritical patterns of degeneracy and worse. And it has been my experience that, before the Crusade event is concluded and the working press has spent some time interviewing Graham and exchanging ideas and questions, the darting eyes vanish and the hardness melts and the set chin and stern glance are gone: for this North Carolinian is real; he is unlike any other celebrity they have known or met.

My relationship with Billy Graham covers some twenty years and some very long distances in theology and biblical studies. It is possible that we still could disagree on some matters.

I came out of a conservative tradition, biblically and prayerfully punctuated. But it was not the fundamentalism which is Billy's platform of personal faith and public preaching. My seminary was Yale and historically it has been a citadel of biblical scholarship with a fierce zeal for pursuing the Christian ethic in every arena of God's creation. Graham's early Crusades (1950) and brash anti-intellectual pronouncements brought a chorus of derision from Yale and from this seminarian at Yale. Our professors shook their heads over his style of mission and ministry. They were all Ivy and he, just another preacher from Backwash Bible.

Despite the jibes and antagonism directed at Billy, a minority of students on our campus indicated an attraction for his public preaching of the gospel to non-Christians and nonbelievers. I mean, who else was doing it? Our ordination vows said that we were to do the work "of an evangelist." While the overwhelming majority of graduates would translate this as preaching the good news of Christ to the poor through identifying with the abused workers, the forgotten field hands, the migrants at the lowest ladder of civilization, the poor and deprived in the urban ghetto through militant advocacy of better laws and true justice and personal compassion, it seemed that the preaching of the Good News, the tackling of a secular, mindless, spiritually empty society, was not high on anyone's agenda. A few in our class were good preachers. Many went on to become outstanding scholars, leaders in college campus ministries, active in social and human welfare, front-runners in governmental and societal reform, and everywhere found in overseas ecumenical programs and experiments. Still, there was a failing, a blind spot, a neglect; every time Graham appeared he was reminding Yale, Harvard, Union, and Princeton seminarians of that gross neglect.

Down deep the mainline churches knew they had overinvested in the social application of the gospel. Certainly it was right and correct and timely. Men and women of daring discipleship and loving nerve put all they had into frightful, even dangerous situations. The world was not worthy of them, and they gave their all. Yet the overcommitment of one dimension of the Christian life, can be distracting and finally dishonest. The inner life, the kingdom of the Spirit, the Good News of Jesus Christ has to be preached as well as lived, spoken as well as served. Graham's ministry soon advanced beyond the regional walls of the Southern revivalism (where mainline liberals longed to label it — and then dismiss it — as quaint and nostalgic and so-o nineteenth century). He was attracting crowds everywhere he went. Even Gotham City with its Fifth Avenue sneer and establishment uneasiness, could not keep Graham out, and a surprising number of "regulars" found that the Word preached was what had been missing — as well as the songs that were sung.

For a while I was content to find a certain amount of Christian expression in the social application of the gospel. The world will never outgrow its need for a corrective stance of the prophets who can, as Somerset Maugham would say, "see through a brick wall." Secular society has come of age, and its fruit has turned millions sour. The Christian probe in politics, government, foreign affairs, civic concerns, and human rights has to be a twenty-four-hour process. Yet nowhere in church history do we find the beloved community pursuing these goals or championing these causes without the equipment and support of a deeply personal faith. There simply is no substitute for Christians to be separated from the source of their faith, the living Christ.

No pronouncements, no group process, no working papers, not even the most articulate creeds can supplant the experience of a soul aflame with the spirit of the risen Christ. Yet to talk about a salvation moment, to communicate personally a redemptive encounter or a pentecostal connection — to speak of this has become downright embarrassing for too many Christians in mainline churches. For me, and apparently for millions of others, Graham provided through his preaching and prayerful appeal the channel of grace that had been misplaced or neglected.

Let me illustrate. In February 1955 I took a group of laymen from upstate New York to a Presbyterian men's meeting in New York. There must have been a dozen of us who set aside four days to attend conferences, workshops, discussions, and great services of singing and praise in the Manhattan Center of New York, near the garment district. Yet, of all the special programming, banquets, and heart-to-heart discussions we sampled, nothing and no one could match the appearance of Billy Graham and the persuasive influence of his message.

I can remember not only what he said, but how he was introduced and what he was wearing (a dark blue sport coat and gray flannel slacks)! He was introduced by the chairman of the meeting, who said simply, "And now here's Billy Graham."

Billy had just returned from England and remembered the difficulty he had with using the correct salutation with titled royalty and ecclesiastical dignitaries. He recalled the incident in a British public school where the headmaster thrilled his student body by telling them the Archbishop of Canterbury would shortly pay them a visit. He cautioned them in saying that the proper address for the august Archbishop was "My Lord" or "Your Grace." Sure enough, the towering cleric arrived, visited with the lads during lunch, and on the way out turned to one fourth-grader and said brightly, "Son, how old are you?" And the youngster, stunned by such attention from such a famous cleric, said, "My God, I'm twelve."

Graham then launched into his sermon-address, speaking without notes but with an open Bible in his hands. He spoke of the necessity and opportunity of being a disciple of Jesus Christ; the thrill and responsibility of such a call; and how life has a way of challenging every personal commitment. He noted that during that very week, *The New York Times* carried an article about the recovery of a list of men who had served with Washington during the long and harsh winter of Valley Forge. There were some fifteen thousand names intact. The historic colonial document revealed that, of the original number, five thousand were disabled through injury and sickness, many suffering death in the field, another five thousand were active enough to campaign, and another five thousand deserted. What was particularly jolting was the evidence that the Defense Department, for the first time, had the names of all the deserters. Graham spoke to the high calling of not deserting Jesus Christ, or not falling by the wayside through some lack of energy or preparation or self-discipline, but having the courage and stamina to follow through to victory.

I suppose by most standards it would have been considered a brief pep talk for the old college try — in this instance, the old, middle-aged crowd that used to attend laity meetings in Manhattan Center. But for me, it was a spiritual reawakening. It had all the charge and challenge of summer conference days where we would have crossed rivers and climbed mountains and scaled peaks for Jesus Christ, if anyone had the audacity to sound the trumpet. I made a prayerful recommitment of my life and ministry as a pastor. Upon returning to my upstate parish, I felt a new glow in the expectations and fulfillment of the gospel of Christ — which I had been ordained to preach and teach several years earlier.

For me, the Graham experience worked in a quiet, resolute manner. I never went forward, never felt the need to sign a decision card or to promote his evangelistic industry by gifts or tithes. Yet, I gained something vital and personal, and so did others. In the next twelve months, almost a hundred new members joined my parish — I'm sure through the confrontation with the Good News that had gained a sharp but personal new edge in my ministry.

THE YEARNING FOR REVIVAL

One of the criticisms aimed at Graham and the Crusade effort of his ministry is the comment that he is a "revivalist." As an evangelist brings good news to those who are totally ignorant of the gospel, revivalists are said to be those who stir and renew what has been lost or diminished in the heart of man. A fair argument can be made that in countless instances Graham is a pure evangelist, claiming a hearing and audience among those who have never known the Christian life and are completely foreign to the saving news of the gospel. To thousands of these, because of his celebrity appeal and fame around the world, Graham has attracted first-time spectators who stayed to make their profession of faith. On the other hand, one *New York Times* study after the New York Crusade of 1957 indicated that nearly 64 percent of those who signed decision cards were in some manner connected with a church or indicated a religious preference. They were not considered "fresh converts" but the fruit of "revivals" held in Madison Square Garden. These facts, according to Graham critics within the Church, nailed him as simply a revivalist.

Perhaps this is the time for people within the Christian Church to make a vigorous defense of the validity of revival and the integrity of the renewing experience of the gospel. In our time, Alexander Solzhenitsyn has called for a revival of Christian values if Russia is to know any justice or integrity in the future:

> In the final analysis the fate of our country, in the true and profound sense, depends on whether the idea of the Rightness of Force becomes finally embedded in the national consciousness, or whether it will be purged by obscurantism and will shine forth again with the FORCE OF RIGHTEOUSNESS. . . .
>
> Shall we succeed in reviving in ourselves, at length some elements of the Christian faith, or are we going to lose the very last of them and abandon ourselves to considerations of self-preservation and personal gain? . . .

We have lost the radiant ethical atmosphere of Christianity in which for a millennium our morals were grounded; we have forfeited our way of life, our outlook on the world, our folklore, even the very name by which the Russian peasant was known. We are losing the last features and marks of a Christian people. . . .[1]

REACHING OUT

A significant factor in Billy's evangelistic success has been his willingness to reach out to the public in almost every possible way. Considering the important persons in our society and the fascination of our mass culture, it is amazing that he has been able to endure the exposure and drain that such an availability entails. We have seen presidents assassinated, movie stars assaulted, and sports heroes mobbed by their fans. It is in the nature of this vastly populated globe for people to want to find identity and belonging with those who have attained a celebrity status and who can, even in a fleeting moment, bring excitement to what they consider a drab, anonymous existence. Sports and political figures have always attracted a crowd in our country. Military and civic heroes gain a following. Motion picture stars add to the clamoring of the public to meet the famous and the fortunate. I remember when Wrong Way Corrigan landed his single-engine plane at a tiny airport in El Paso, Texas. He had gained notoriety by flying across the ocean (without federal clearance for his flight in such a marginally equipped aircraft) and landing successfully in Europe. He said that it was the result of a miscalculation: he was really heading for Des Moines or somewhere, and surprisingly found himself on another continent. "Wrong Way Corrigan" was the term that stuck, and our high school gang was out there to welcome him to West Texas. For at least an afternoon he had more status and adulation than a Texas Ranger.

I mention this excitement and strain as a modest preamble to the pressure and ballyhoo that has accompanied Billy Graham during his more than twenty-five years in public ministry. By the very nature of his mission, he has gone after the public, searched out the masses, reached out to the man and woman on the street corners and byways. To give of oneself to a hundred thousand people in a stadium, to spend hour by hour in taping studios for television shows, to arrange an hour or two or three every day on the road being interviewed by the press and photographed by the news media — this is to endure what can be described only as a physical and mental beating. Yet Billy has been able to sustain this pace and satisfy the normal needs of an inquiring civilization out of his love for Christ and his hope that, through his preaching and conversation, the gospel may be real and lasting to more and more people.

REACHING OUT — BUT THERE ARE LIMITS

The availability of Billy Graham must be counted as one of the solid reasons for his international influence. He is better known and more widely respected than any other Christian leader and probably any other religious leader of any faith because of his accessibility and openness. On the several occasions that we have been together during the past decade, being exposed to crowds in Europe, in Washington, New York, Philadelphia, he was never restrained or hesitant about meeting and visiting with the public and the usual request to sign an autograph or pray for someone in trouble. During the height of the New York and London Crusades, there were times when he had to take his meals in his hotel room in order to have time to eat without interruption. Yet he always seemed to know that the stranger, the waitress, the cab driver, the teen-age kids running after him really had needs that were deeper than his fame and more pressing than a personal desire to preserve his privacy.

BUT NOT ALWAYS AVAILABLE

In the tumult of the sixties, the religious ferment in the American scene brought a celebrity status to many who were active in church leadership. The civil rights movement and the antiwar campaign by churchmen, along with the urgency for reform within the Roman Catholic Church, brought religious issues to the focus of mass media. Many of their personalities were good writers, clever conversationalists, and sometimes outrageous in their suggestions for an immediate acceptance of the New Morality. Of all major publishers, Hugh Hefner of *Playboy* magazine seemed most prepared to exploit and extend this mood of irreverence within the church. (In fact, it was widely known that Hefner had urged the seminaries to teach his *Playboy* ethics as the coming style of the Christian life; it was not true that he offered to endow a chair at a major seminary. He did, for more than a decade, offer a special discount for clergy subscribers.)

During the sixties *Playboy* was terribly avant-garde, at least for the middle-aged readers, and Hefner was dealing out his *Playboy* philosophy, not by the line but by the yard in each issue. His *Playboy* interviews were often as not an article about some religious personality with an axe to grind or a cause to promote.

In 1969, during the height of Hefner's influence, Theodore Roszak came along and scathingly destroyed the *Playboy* philosophy, intellectually dissembling what Billy had already discarded as false and fabricated morality. Roszak wrote:

> The *Playboy* version of total permissiveness . . . now imposes its image upon us in every slick movie and posh magazine that comes along. In the affluent society, we have sex and sex galore — or so we are to believe. But when we look more closely, we see that this Sybaritic promiscuity wears a special social coloring. It has been assimilated to an income level and social status available only to our well-heeled junior executives and the jet set. After all, what does it cost to rent these yachts full of nymphomaniacal young things in which our playboys sail off to orgiastic swimming parties in the Bahamas? *Real* sex, we are led to believe, is something that goes with the best scotch, twenty-seven-dollar sunglasses and platinum-tipped shoelaces. Anything less is a shabby substitute.[2]

Liberal clergymen, frequently former priests, and often a Bishop Pike were given the spotlight between the centerfold and some lewd cartoon. Hefner was having a field day. His ancient animosity toward organized religion in general and Christianity in particular was given full vent. Aside from the magazine attention to clergy types who espoused his sentiments, Hefner invited the really relaxed clerics to his mansion in Chicago, complete with bunnies, old movies, and the inevitable Pepsi-Cola.

As satisfying as this was to Hefner, he failed in his grand design:

to make a fool out of Graham. He believed that since so many name clergy were in his book or on his invitation list, surely Billy would be more than eager to have this terrific limelight. Yet Graham knew where Hefner stood, and it was a moral quicksand that not only is now engulfing the aging publisher but has destroyed many around him. (A few years ago Hefner's personal secretary committed suicide just prior to a police investigation.) Money was no barrier. After a series of inquiries, Hefner finally offered Graham $25,000 for a single story. Negative. Billy was reaching out, but not at the expense of being identified with one of the heavy promoters of the "enemies" list.

A couple of years ago, Billy Graham and his team were in the Miami airport. Hugh Hefner happened to be there, complete with handlers, agents, and bunnies, headed for some resort in the Caribbean. Hefner rushed across the lobby to greet the evangelist and with that certain, sly aggressiveness began to pump Billy's hand while several of his scantily clad bunnies quietly stepped behind them, creating a rather downhill backdrop. But just as swiftly, Billy's associates Grady Wilson and George Beverly Shea stepped in front of the lovelies. The prize picture turned out to be Graham and team talking to a bewildered Hefner. It would not surprise this writer that before the end of this decade, Hefner will make a personal attempt to reach Graham and to gain some fragment of personal salvation from a man he could never manipulate or coerce. Hefner is in big trouble in River City.

When Billy was sponsored for a major urban campaign in the new Madison Square Garden, he spent one evening describing the shame and filth of Times Square. In fact, the entire day before, he had put on his now famous disguise of mustache and pork-pie hat and quietly pounded the pavements of the West Side, noting the skin flicks, the newly created massage parlors, the thriving pornographic playhouses which were jammed with Middle America. Said Billy the following night:

> I was absolutely overwhelmed by the openness and depth of sin that I saw in Times Square. [3]

Many New Yorkers shrugged it off as Graham's not understanding the natural pleasures of Gotham City and his overpersuasion of conservative Christian ethics. But Roszak's writing indicated that there were some who understood, sensed the disease stealthily at work, and identified the enemy:

> *Playboy* sexuality is, ideally, casual, frolicsome, and vastly promiscuous. It is the anonymous sex of the harem. It creates no binding loyalties, no personal attachments, no distractions from one's primary responsibilities — which are to the company, to one's career and social position, and to the system generally. The perfect playboy practices a career enveloped by noncommittal trivialities: there is no home, no family, no romance that divides the heart painfully. . . . *Playboy* gives us a conception of femininity which is indistinguishable from social idiocy. The woman becomes a mere playmate, a submissive bunny, a mindless decoration.[4]

Now, nearly a decade later, it appears that the condescending New Yorkers are prepared to agree that Graham was correct in his forthright attack on the pornography disease of midtown Manhattan. Indeed, the epidemic has spread to every midtown in the nation, fueled by the unlimited resources of the underworld and surely prepared by the slick permissiveness of *Playboy* and its huckster pack. Graham's unshakable, almost iron-framed conservative stance in this matter was long derided by liberal Christians and openly mocked by secular critics. Today's wreckage in the lives and reputations of so many of these people gives an obvious judgment on who was right and who was sadly misled. The sexual permissiveness and new morality that flourished so confidently and popularly in the sixties has revealed tragic decay a decade later. Graham became number one in the Christian world leadership role out of his fidelity to what he believed and his unwavering determination to remain with it when others were caught up in fads and passing ethical styles.

THE SUCCESS OF *MY ANSWER*

Beyond the influence and outreach of the television and radio ministry of the Graham organization is the daily newspaper column written by the evangelist. The printed word has always had enormous reach, and such religious writers as Bishop Fulton J.

Sheen and Norman Vincent Peale continue to demonstrate the effects of such a column. Billy's columns appear all over the world. The success of this venture lies in a combination of candor and personal touch. A careful survey of his topics and themes reveals a commitment to making his material personal and supportive. In Great Britain in the summer of 1969, Dr. Graham dealt in the press with the problems of youth, the irritation of a regular attending church member, and the guilt of an individual worried over the failure to live up to high aspirations — and all in one week.

A young person wrote to the evangelist:

> I am a teenager and became a Christian a year ago. I am discouraged, even though I pray, as my family are not Christians. Can you help me?[5]

Graham's reply was,

> First, let me congratulate you on taking a stand for Christ, even though home conditions seem unfavourable at the moment.
> What you are experiencing is perfectly natural. The Bible doesn't promise that following Christ is an easy way. Christ said, "If any man would come after me, let him deny himself, and take up his cross and follow me."
> You say you are discouraged. Discouragement is one of Satan's tools. Your family is watching you, and if you are faithful you can be the means of winning them to Christ.
> Remember faithfulness is one of the crowning Christian virtues. Jesus said to a man who had been faithful: "Thou has been faithful over a few things, I will make thee ruler over many things; enter thou into the joy of thy Lord."
> You are probably on the verge of a real triumph, but if you fall a prey to discouragement and give up, you will never know the joy which is promised to the faithful. Say these words over and over: "I can do all things through Christ, who strengtheneth me." They are true and will never fail.
> Christ needs young people like you to offset the tide of flippancy and delinquency among our youth. Don't let Him down.[6]

Another reader asked,

> Is it wise to change to another church?[7]

This topic must have attracted as much clergy attention as laity readership. . . .

> I wouldn't recommend changing churches, for I have a feeling that your reaction to the sermons of a new minister would be similar. You see, to enjoy anything, we must have a lively interest in it.
> What are your true interests? Clothes? Art? Music? Sports? I dare say that if your minister spent twenty minutes talking on a subject close to your heart that you would give close attention.
> Begin to school yourself in the Scriptures. Develop an ear and appetite for spiritual things. And pray also for the fullness of the Spirit of God in your life. "When He is come, He will reveal unto you all truth."
> Having said that, I would like to remind all clergymen that Jesus was a simple preacher. . . . His method of preaching was simple. . . . He preached with authority. . . . He was repetitious.
> James Denney, the great Scottish theologian, once said: "If you shoot over the head of your hearers you don't prove anything except that you don't know how to shoot."[8]

Another person was worried about past sins, asking the American evangelist,

> I can't stop worrying about my sins even though I am sorry about them and have confessed them to God. What can I do?[9]

Billy responded,

> There is a great difference between remorse and repentance. The lives of many people are filled with remorse because they know that their past actions have brought grief to others. The Bible tells us, 2 Corinthians 7:9, about being "made sorry." The sorrow which God uses means a change of heart that leads to salvation — it is the world's sorrow that is such a deadly thing.
> When this happens as a result of some sinful act, we are then ready to turn to Christ and accept the pardon that He offers. If you have done that and if you still continue to worry about sins, it is because you have not yet believed what the Bible says about the whole matter.
> The Bible clearly tells us, Romans 3:24, Phillips Translation, that "a man who has faith is now freely acquitted in the eyes of God by his generous dealing in the Redemptive Act of Jesus Christ." This is what you must receive in simple faith. Only then will your worrying come to an end.
> Satan likes nothing better than to remind us of our past sins.[10]

Finally, another writer stated,

> I make so many good resolves, especially at each New Year, but
> somehow I don't keep them. I want to be a good disciple of Christ,
> well-versed in the Scriptures, and dedicated to His cause. But, I
> find myself falling short of these high resolves. Have you any
> suggestions?[11]

Answer:

Yes, I have! Make a resolution to keep your resolutions!

Good resolutions which cross the mind fleetingly dissolve and
come to naught. Disraeli, the great prime minister of England,
once said: "The secret of success is constancy of purpose." My wife
has written over the work table in our kitchen: "Work and pray and
peg away."

Have a definite goal and work toward it. An obese friend of mine
printed this motto and stuck it to his refrigerator door: "Lose five
pounds this month"; and he did. I heard of a woman who became
disgusted with her nagging, and wrote a note to herself, "This year
I'm going to become the best wife in the world," and her husband
fell in love with her all over again. Set a definite goal for your
devotional life such as: "I'm going to read five chapters of the Bible
every day, and talk to the Lord for fifteen minutes." Then, live up
to this goal.

Paul said, "This one thing I do," and he became a legend in his
time. God has little in store for those who do not aim at something
high, and press toward it. Haphazard living does not become a
dedicated Christian but noble purpose is the mark of Christ's
disciples.[12]

CHAPTER 4

The Fame Game

The Fame Game

The dismay of the fifties had turned to the disasters of the sixties. But Billy was there with a message of hope and fulfillment. Although his preaching was full of warnings and signs of alarm and apprehension, he took a public stance quite the opposite of the secular doomsday prophets. And for many of them, distinguished and pensive, the bad news had been evident for a long time.

During World War II one of the individuals who brought the conflict overseas close to the American citizen was a reporter named Ernie Pyle. His coverage of the active fighting of American armed forces overseas made the war both vivid and personal to many American families. His writings have become almost a journal of what the American GI did in Europe and Asia. He always seemed to be a part of the men with whom he visited and later wrote about. He suffered with them. He saw their wounds. He knew their defeats as well as their successes. And yet of himself, he once wrote that the most difficult time of the war for him was not when he was at the fighting front or in the difficult days of the bombing of London. His most desperate hour was the moment when he was in a hotel room in London and received the word of the death of his mother in America. Here, in the quietness of his own room, separated by such great distance from his Stateside family, he had to wrestle with the ultimate questions of life. And in that encounter he confessed that he could find no answer. And so he wrote:

> It seems to me that life is futile, and death the final indignity. People live and suffer and grow bent with yearning, bowed with disappointment and then they die and what is it all for? I do not know. [1]

That was the searching, searing question that Ernie Pyle had asked of himself and in a way is asking of you and me. He was killed during the war and never really found release from this despair against life.

Modern writers of both the stage and fiction have steadily expressed their concern about life — if not frustration and torment, then despair. Tennessee Williams, who has been applauded and damned alike by theater-goers, has one of his characters in *Sweet Bird of Youth* called the "Heckler." At one point the Heckler comes to center stage and offers a word which will explain the dreary lives that are portrayed in this play. He says,

> I believe that the silence of God, the absolute speechlessness of Him, is a long, long and awful thing. The world has lost because of it. I think it is yet to be broken to any man or any human who yet lived on earth, no exceptions.

Williams sees the world and the dreary lives of what he called the silence of God, the absolute speechlessness of Him.

Contemporary poet, Dylan Thomas, promoting his own atheism and concerned about his father's growing pious on his deathbed, said to him,

> Do not go gentle into that good night,
> Old age should burn and rave at close of day;
> Rage, rage, against the dying of the light.

Graham was able to answer this mood by presenting a vivid picture of a God who was not only Creator of the past, but also Lord of the present and future. While his biblicism irritated many scholars and his absolutist statements confounded liberal Christian philosophers, he gained enormous following from millions, for he affirmed that for the faithful, life would not only work out now, but ultimately, in a glorious coming of Jesus Christ at the end of the age.

So while Arthur Koestler was inquiring of modern man,

> Is history a mad river at flood stage sweeping all before it, leaving people and institutions piles like debris on the sand-bars of strife or drowned in the eddies of intrigue? Or is history a purposeful unfolding of God's will?[2]

the North Carolina preacher was declaring the marvelous works of God soon to be fulfilled in a divine plan.

DOING THE ONE THING WELL

When identifying the achievements of a person such as Billy Graham, it is helpful at times to balance the list by reporting opportunities which were rejected, turned aside, postponed, or undeveloped. Our lives are shaped frequently by what is not done or followed, as much as the single goal pursued and sustained.

Through my friendship with Billy (as well as his closeness to those in my family), I have seen distinct topics considered and then turned aside, primarily because they did not fit the special skills that he believed God had given him. Over and over again he would tell those who approached him with special interests, projects, or promotions, that "God has called me to preach and to feed His flock," and with that, firmly say no to the most intensive persuasions imaginable.

There were the classic and proper enticements that would satisfy any young man with poise and stature: the movies; politics; sports; and creating a major university. (The two major related industries that he did enter were closely identified with the evangelistic thrust of the Crusades: creation with his father-in-law, Nelson Bell, of the journal, *Christianity Today*; and the sponsorship of feature films with biblical themes, as well as the Graham films shown at the New York World's Fair in 1964.)

His fascination with sports was an early and natural option for

Billy. He was outstanding in several sports in high school and college, and many in the family circle wondered if some professional baseball club might sign him up because of his athletic talents.

When one tallies the number of clergymen's sons in the movies, theater, and show business, it is not surprising that Graham should have had a major opportunity for stardom: David Hartman, John Davidson, and David Frost (to name just a few). Early in his public career as an evangelist, Billy was referred to in *Look* as the "Barrymore of the pulpit."[3] Actors' skills of communication and persuasion are present in most preachers. The use of emotion, the clarity of pronunciation, and the sense of timing are regular trademarks of any major evangelist throughout Christian history. The New Testament is draped with Paul's vivid public proclamations; church history reveals a fiery Knox, an eloquent Wesley, and a barn-burning style of Jonathan Edwards.

In those Los Angeles nights, Graham's handsome profile and elegant style captured the attention of a Hollywood producer. Paul Short remembers —

> I know from personal experience: Billy Graham is the man whose personality and example gave me an understanding and appreciation of the Christian life which I never before realized could actually be possible. Naturally, I recognized the Graham impact generally, but it never occurred to me that it would ever become a personal matter with me.
>
> It all started when I was under contract to a major Hollywood motion picture studio as a writer-producer, following my discharge from the Naval Air Corps in 1946.
>
> I had never met Billy Graham and actually had heard little of him. Although I attended various churches regularly, I had never affiliated myself with any specific church. This had never bothered me particularly since I considered myself a good man. Was I not kind, generous, and did I not at all times avoid evil in any form? I also considered myself a happy and well-adjusted person.
>
> How sad it is and how regrettable that thousands feel the same way and therefore miss, sometimes forever, the true peace and joy that can come only by living the Christian life with active participation in a Church program.
>
> When I assumed my Hollywood post, I was aware that the major studios there had long been acutely interested in the intensely

moving story of a young minister as told in *The Gauntlet* by James Street. I also knew that production of this story had been halted because of the unavailability of the exact type of leading man as demanded by the leading role. None of the talented actors in the film capitol could quite measure up to the part.

I quickly became fascinated with the search for the right person and subsequently found myself devoting all of my spare time between my own writing and producing assignments to a sort of private search of my own for this very special individual.

In 1949 Los Angeles newspapers began carrying brief stories about a young evangelist who had opened a revival meeting in the city. The stories became increasingly important daily as more and more space was allotted to a Dr. Billy Graham.

Los Angeles newspapers, among the best in the nation, are not exactly famous for their generosity in giving space unless the subject matter is of especial interest and importance, newsworthy-wise, yet the Graham headlines became bigger and bigger and more glowing with each day. Photographs revealed a young and handsome man with a verve and zeal that projected through the newspaper cameras.

This surely must be the ideal man we're all looking for to play the important "Gauntlet" role, I told myself, and I lost no time in rushing down town to the tented enclosure where the revival was being held. My wife and I drove for more than an hour before we could find a place to park — blocks away from the tent. We finally made our way through the standing throng of people at the tent's edge.

We were spellbound!

At the close of the service I was able to arrange a personal interview with Dr. Graham for the next day. I returned to the studio in a special state of excitement and was told to let the young evangelist name his own salary and terms if he would accept the role in the picture.

I confess I was so elated about the possibilities of the young man playing the role that I completely overlooked the tremendous work he was doing in his own field. I looked forward with great excitement to the interview. I was totally unprepared for what took place.

Refusal — just plain, flat refusal!

This is incredible, I told myself. Young, handsome and perfect-for-the-part, Dr. Graham was gentle; he was sincere; he was appreciative, but he wanted nothing other than to be free to preach. He was gracious but he also was not in the least impressed by the idea or the unprecedented motion picture offer.

Although the shock was of the delayed reaction type to me, I came away from that interview with the certain realization that I had been talking to one of the really great men of all time and one of the most dedicated.[4]

Billy's name has surfaced with election year regularity. Since Eisenhower days he has been mentioned as a presidential candidate. Once a movement was afoot to run him for the Senate from North Carolina: nothing much happened. In 1972 rumors flourished, until he firmly denied that he would be a candidate for the White House. Whatever his private reasons (and good sense), he has never encouraged the enthusiasm of followers who write in his name or propose a ticket with him on board.

Christian education presented a different, more complicated question, especially in the consideration of starting a Crusade University. Next to starting a church, building a church college seems to be a favorite calling of many Christian leaders. My grandfather built churches all over Oregon, but I am sure that his greatest satisfaction were the two or three colleges he founded that had a Christian vision at the center. In 1959-60 Billy became part of a serious effort to establish a Christian university in New Jersey. His travels about the country revealed the soaring demand for student enrollment, particularly in a Christian environment.

In pursuing support for such a major educational endeavor (beginning costs were to be in excess of $18 million), Billy sent this letter to a select group of interested and wealthy friends:

BILLY GRAHAM
September 1959

Dear Friends;

For some years the Lord has been laying upon my heart and upon the hearts of some of my friends the need in America for a truly Christian university. I thank God for the many fine Christian colleges, Bible schools, seminaries, and elementary and secondary schools in America today. These are doing a fine work and are certainly worthy of the support of God's people. In most cases, they are carrying a maximum load, often with limited facilities and support.

I am not an educator and have no intention of entering that field. God has called me to preach and to "feed His flock." I have, however, sensed the need of an institution that would supplement the work now being done in the field of higher education. Many evangelical schools are already turning away students, and according to national studies, we are about to enter upon a period of unprecedented growth in higher education. On the basis of population studies, college enrollments are scheduled to increase 100% during the next ten years. What an opportunity! What a challenge!

More than half of the young people in the United States are now being trained in state institutions and the proportion is increasing each year. There is urgent need for additional facilities on the undergraduate and graduate levels on the part of private institutions if we are to maintain a proper balance and insure the American way of life. I believe that as Christians we should seek to provide Christian training in every area for our young people as we are admonished to do in the Word of God. One of the crying needs today in higher education is the need for graduate as well as undergraduate training based on a Christian philosophy.

The Lord has placed the burden for such an institution upon the hearts of some of my friends, and I have agreed to do what I could to bring together plans and people so that together we might build to the glory of God.

In the following pages we shall endeavor to present briefly and clearly what we have in mind. I pray that your heart may be moved, as has mine, and that I may have the joy of hearing that you will join us in making this dream a reality.

Cordially yours,

Billy Graham

Several important, high-level meetings were held in Washington and New York during 1959-60. Christian leaders such as my uncle, Dan Poling, of the *Christian Herald,* Carl Henry of *Christianity Today,* Harold Ockenga of Boston, Nelson Bell from Montreat, and a core group of Wheaton College administration and faculty did most of the planning. The really big guns, such as Howard Pew of Sun Oil, Stanley S. Kresge, Sr., of 5 & 10 cent store fame, New York business tycoons Roger Hull and George Champion, and Texan Howard Butt, Jr., were invited to share in the initial discussions of the feasibility of such a proposal.

This group had already studied the doctrinal platform, which came from the heart of fundamentalism:

> The trustees and faculty will be asked to subscribe to the following statement of faith:
>
> We believe in the Scriptures of the Old and the New Testaments as inspired by God and inerrant in the original writing, and that they are of supreme and final authority in faith and life.
>
> We believe in one God, eternally existing in three persons: Father, Son, and Holy Spirit.
>
> We believe that Jesus Christ was begotten by the Holy Spirit, born of the Virgin Mary, and is true God and true man.
>
> We believe that man was created in the image of God; that he sinned, and thereby incurred, not only physical death, but also that spiritual death which is separation from God; and that all human beings are born with a sinful nature, and, in the case of those who reach moral responsibility, become sinners in thought, word, and deed.
>
> We believe that the Lord Jesus Christ died for our sins, according to the Scriptures, as a representative and substitutionary sacrifice; and that all who believe in Him are justified on the ground of His shed blood.
>
> We believe in the resurrection of the crucified body of our Lord, in His ascension into heaven, and in His present life there for us, as High Priest and Advocate.
>
> We believe in "that blessed hope," the personal and imminent return of our Lord and Saviour, Jesus Christ.
>
> We believe that all who receive by faith the Lord Jesus Christ are born again of the Holy Spirit, and thereby become children of God.
>
> We believe in the bodily resurrection of the just and the unjust, the everlasting blessedness of the saved, and the everlasting punishment of the lost.

This statement did not appear to cause any large problems for the group. Negativism *may* have been stirred by the speech given by Enoch Dyrness, Registrar of Wheaton, who told the potential donors and sponsors at a meeting in New York:

> Personally I am convinced that we must not compromise in matters of faith and life. If this institution is to maintain distinctive objectives, it will be necessary for all connected with it — trustees, faculty, staff, and students — to live so as to honor our Lord and

Savior Jesus Christ. By that I mean that we must be ready to pay the price of being different from the world. Worldly practices such as smoking, drinking, gambling, dancing, and theater attendance are not conducive to spiritual growth and should not be a part of campus life. I am not saying that a person could not be a Christian and do some of these things, but I am firmly convinced, and the record will bear me out, that it has been at this point that many colleges and universities founded as Christian institutions have lost their spiritual fervor. After 100 years, we at Wheaton are convinced that separation from worldly practices is a price that must be paid if the spiritual life of the institution is to be maintained. There will need to be agreement at this point. An orthodox doctrinal statement is not enough.

Billy began to realize that an Eastern reflection of Wheaton would not sell. Even calling it Crusade University did not have the clout to transfer loyalty and support from his evangelistic success to a university setting. Almost everyone around the table in Roger Hull's office had a school or college to take care of — some, several. Many of them, such as Dan Poling, were active trustees on other church college boards. Billy's proposal for another church college gave many of them a queasy feeling in the stomach. The biggest potential donor, Howard Pew, was already a generous supporter of evangelistic crusades led by Graham; more than this, he had underwritten the first decade of red ink for *Christianity Today*. So when the educational theme came forward, Pew must have had visions of the millions he was already pouring in Grove City College. One school was enough.

On another level, even these orthodox, conservative Christians were passing through social, ethical, and moral accommodations to Western civilization called America. Billy knew this, and the proposal of such a severe campus standard of personal conduct was unreal, no matter what the model, Wheaton, proved on the plains of Illinois. One of the participants of the first discussions for Crusade University, my Uncle Dan, shared many of Billy's feelings about the need for dynamic Christian witness of the college campus. He had served as trustee on the boards of several Christian colleges and was soon to assist in the revival of Conwell Seminary in Philadelphia. But his years of experience with "worldly Christians" (including his multimillionaire brother-in-law who enjoyed good scotch and flashy limousines and Long Island estates) had informed him personally that they would give generously to vital spiritual movements but were hesitant on this project.

Assembled around the table were those who had eagerly and generously supported Billy in his great Crusades: Champion, Hill, wise and wily Howard Pew. Yet each of these men moved in a stratosphere of the private club, the swank social organizations, the society of champagne receptions with white shoes and Havanna cigars. The pronouncement of a Wheaton "social formula" (as Uncle Dan later identified it) just did not get off the ground. It did not diminish Billy's standing with these captains of industry; indeed, they all increased their support of ensuing Crusades in the United States and overseas. But the strategy of evangelism (and their affection for Billy) was not transferable to an education venture.

Billy knew that the ground was shifting. It had for him, and it had for us. We never read Sunday newspapers as children; we did not permit "funnies" to be in the house on Sunday morning. We never thought, even, of attending a movie on Sunday. . . it never entered our mind. The Sabbath alterations hit us all, probably more quickly with the advent of television. At a dinner at the Union League Club with the Polings, Billy was asked by my Aunt Lillian (glaring at Dan), "What do you think of a Christian minister who comes home after Sunday worship and camps in front of the television, watching professional football the rest of the day?" Billy smiled and said quietly, "Not much, Mrs. Poling, and that's just what I do myself!"

The college crises changed, from soaring enrollment to declining student bodies in a short fifteen years. Graham was probably saved by his friends from a major economic disaster.

CHAPTER 5

What the Evangelist Tells His Friends

What the Evangelist Tells His Friends

During a Crusade in Arizona I visited Billy on a rare day off. He was staying at the Casa Blanca Inn, and his outfit that morning suggested the attire fit for the sporting activities of Scottsdale. Here at this desert oasis one catches a glimpse of the upper echelon of American business and professional life. The winter air is gentle, the sun hot. People from all over North America gather at the watering places located at Palm Springs, Tucson, and Phoenix.

Billy looks tan and tired. (The golfing score is secret but his sweat is public, and he laughs about his early morning golf disaster.) He looks taller and his hair is getting gray to white and the smile seems more swift and the eyes more intense.

A decade ago Ted Fiske of *The New York Times* interviewed Billy in North Carolina and said that he was amazed at the intensity of Billy's glance — "like you were the only person that existed in the world at that time."

Billy moves around this resort suite with a lanky, relaxed grace, never awkward, and today he shifts like a basketball player who is taking a few moments out for halftime.

75

Always it is a pause or time-out when I have been with Billy. We are away from the stadium or arena or TV studio or church meeting. The first time we met was at a dinner in Philadelphia. Dan Poling and I were at the banquet to promote the future of Conwell Seminary, a project close to my uncle's heart, and to honor the famous churchman who founded Temple University after his preaching success at the Baptist Temple in the 1800s. Billy was the principal speaker that night. All his energy and persuasion was employed to influence that guest list of two hundred to support an evangelical seminary of urban concern. Dan was pleased that later in the evening Howard Pew, after meeting with Billy and himself, had pledged a sizeable amount to launch the project. It could not have happened without Billy: the crowd was there to meet and hear him. Pew had known Dan and believed in Graham, and this combination worked forcefully and persuasively with the multimillionaire head of Sun Oil.

I learned something about Billy that evening which has stayed fresh for years: his loyalty and support of friends. It is a quality that marks a person, no matter where one finds himself in life. If we cannot love and support friends, where shall we put our investment of life and living? Billy had taken a day train from Washington, and late that evening or early the next morning would be flying out for a Crusade in Brazil or who knows where — yet he squeezed into his schedule the keeping of this date and the sharing of his influence with a leading donor to Christian causes. It was his way of responding to the friendship that Dan Poling had given him in his early days. Dan would say to critics of Billy at the *Christian Herald*, "I know you can't always agree or maybe always support him, but just remember, he's our boy." I never understood that phrase until I understood the loyalties and sincerity of Graham's friendship with Dan Poling

Billy and I sipped an iced tea as we looked across the broad campus of this resort in the desert. Our thoughts were forced from Scottsdale to San Clemente. Billy had a deep, almost dark expression on his face as we spoke of Richard Nixon.

"Do you know," he said, "do you know that we have really been friends for more than twenty years? I mean friends, not just an evangelist with his picture being taken with the President at the White House. We even go to his daughters' birthday parties."

He was leading up to something, and then it broke: "I can't believe those tapes."

When the transcripts of the White House tapes were released, Billy was startled and shocked. In fact, the day the transcripts were published, Graham received a call from the President of the United States apologizing for the vulgarity and profanity of Richard M. Nixon. Nixon knew, after twenty years of golfing, birthday parties, and Florida vacations that Billy Graham is one of those truly authentic Christians who do not swear, do not permit staff or members of their family to use profanity, and expect the same deportment of those in public office. Billy spoke about the college humor and salty language of Kennedy, the stall and corral language of Johnson and Truman — but Nixon . . .

Graham suffered through the Watergate disaster. He was angry at the cover-up formula and distressed to find so many people in public life that were using the White House for unfair and unchristian acts to support a President. Yet in all the aftermath and turmoil and shame that followed the Nixons into a San Clemente exile, Graham has never turned his back on Richard Nixon and remains his supporting friend today. To have Billy Graham as a friend is to have a friend in and out of season.

To understand the sickening drama and sharp heartaches that touched Billy so personally during the Watergate era (and the presidential collapse that followed), you need only to recall the friendship between these men and the affection they shared for each other in the early sixties.

The Nixon-Kennedy contest had been terribly close, and in the final count Nixon lost by only 119,000 votes. Many influential Republicans had urged Billy to give some sort of endorsement to his friend, their candidate. Norman Vincent Peale and Dan Poling early in the campaign had challenged Kennedy's effectiveness in the White House and ability to withstand Vatican persuasions. And while the Protestant community did not vote a religious preference in the election, active Republicans knew of Graham's fondness of Eisenhower and thought it only logical that the evangelist would say *something* in favor of Nixon.

Yet even twenty years ago Billy began to feel called to a larger place in the affairs of this country — and that larger place was Christian leadership touching all parties and every race, not confined to a region or even a theological stance. He demurred and resisted the pleading for a Nixon endorsement.

In the closing weeks of the presidential contest Henry Luce of the powerful *Time-Life-Fortune-Sports Illustrated* publishing empire persuaded Billy to write a supportive piece for *Life* magazine. Even when completed, Billy fretted — then became alarmed at his action and went into a period of prayer and deep soul-searching. The rumor channels went to work, and Democratic politicians called to express their anxiety and apprehension over his proposed article. For reasons of his own, Luce pulled the piece moments before going to press and informed Billy at the last minute that the article had been killed. "I'm so relieved, I feel like shouting," responded the evangelist.

Later on Nixon felt like screaming. The election had been lost by the tiniest fraction of votes. Many in his circle of advisors and friends believed that the *Life* piece by Billy would have put Nixon in the White House. It was a sighing, regretful period for both men.

On January 21, 1969, when Nixon had at last won and was being inaugurated, Graham was the personal platform guest of the new President and offered the dedicatory prayer. Hopes for this struggling, scrambling California Quaker seemed most promising and, to Billy, most exciting. To the press he stated:

> I have known him for many years and after many conversations with him, I am convinced that his greatest concern is that America shall have a moral and spiritual renewal.

In late September, 1973, when the Watergate commotion had become a frenzy, Graham became an easy target for the liberal press. Wanting to sort out some of the evasive issues, I wrote in my syndicated column:

Putting the Blame on Billy Graham

Watergate has a way of touching every aspect of American life. Church, college, and community affairs that turn sour or reveal bad decisions are called "mini-Watergates." Individuals and groups tagged with failure are labelled "plumbers." Even phrases and sentences such as "one thing is perfectly clear" and "at that point in time" must be linked with double meanings or not used at all.

The religious community has churned the Watergate episode to a holy froth. Liberals are blaming White House establishment religious leaders, such as Billy Graham, for the morality that made Watergate possible. Graham, writing in *The New York Times,* argued that the spiritual and moral collapse of the whole country — especially the permissiveness of the sixties — was the source of the political plotting. James A. Michener responding to Graham's statement in the same newspaper exploded with:

> "He has it backwards. The men who engineered Watergate were the least permissive in America. They sat Sunday mornings in the White House and listened to Billy Graham himself preach consoling approval of the status quo. He was one of the few men in America who could have influenced the course of Watergate, and he did nothing about it."

The difficulty here is our short memory and limited information concerning the workings of the White House. In fact, the Sunday services were the dream of the Secret Service who wanted the President out of sanctuary target areas. This suited Mr. Nixon, as his religious persuasions were vague and most personal. Most of the time he is at San Clemente, California, or Florida — White House Services, when held, were for senior members of the administration and family. Graham, Dr. Peale, and others were on the invitational list of preachers.

The conservative religious theme has been a close one to our most recent Presidents. And critics have been eager to lay the blame on Billy Graham for his advisor, companion role to Johnson and Nixon (and he was very close to Eisenhower). Yet many who sit in judgment on the evangelist and his role do not have the back-stage perspective, and their memories are failing on even public accounts. Consider the war in Vietnam. Graham did give tacit approval to the conflict by supporting the Johnson-Nixon participation — and certainly, the bombing. Yet it was Billy Graham who exerted every influence to place Senator Mark Hatfield as the Vice-President on the Nixon slate in 1968 — the leading Republican *critic* of the Asian policy.

Graham holds the heartache, shock, disappointment, and shame of the Watergate tragedy to himself. He stays in touch with the former President and offers advice and assistance to the family and their young people. While the wolves continue to howl for the hide of Richard Nixon, the evangelist remains his personal friend. Yet the downfall of the Nixon administration and the moral collapse that surrounded so many of his aides is only a fresh reminder to Billy that we are all sinners in desperate, urgent need of the saving power of Jesus Christ.

Several years ago I arranged a luncheon between Billy and the famous medal sculptor, Ralph Menconi. The outcome of that meeting changed my attitude toward Graham from candid critic to enthusiastic interpreter.

Ralph Menconi had discussed with me his desire to sculpt a series of art medals of the World's Great Religions. He was at the height of his career, having completed his historic series of the Presidents of the United States — and *Time* had just used his Nixon medal for a cover illustration. And Ralph had acquired a deep interest in the symbolism and philosophy of man's search for God. His stained-glass windows were recently dedicated in a Lutheran Church in Pleasantville, New York, causing a very favorable discussion in that Westchester community. He yearned to extend his art by doing the personalities that shaped man's religious history: Moses, Paul, Luther, Calvin, and others.

In preparing for the series Menconi invited me to gather a panel of world religious leaders to act as an advisory committee and share in the selection of appropriate symbols and design. It was a large order. But men and women of faith responded enthusiastically to the project, among them personalities such as Bishop Sheen, Norman Peale, David Ben-Gurion, and Billy Graham.

When it came time to discuss the Baptist Medal, Billy suggested a meeting in Washington, D.C., and we met for lunch at the Mayflower Hotel. For several hours we went over the material that Ralph had prepared. Billy and Ruth offered comments and suggestions, but generally were awed (as were most people) with the intensity and force of Menconi's work. (At this meeting his Baptist medals were in clay.)

During lunch Billy and I discussed some tender topics. He had long been a supporter of our forces in Southeast Asia and believed he must not falter in backing President Nixon in his plan to complete the war in Vietnam with justice. Just when it appeared that negotiations might settle the conflict, Nixon had ordered the bombing of Cambodia and seemed on the brink of extending the war into a whole new chapter of death and destruction. While not arguing with Billy on his stand, I sensed that he was deeply troubled over the extension of the war and the severity of its effect on the civilian population of North and South Vietnam.

Then Billy said abruptly, "What can people expect me to do? March in protest? Carry a sign? If I do that, then all the doors at the White House and all the avenues to people in high office in this administration are closed to me." He then revealed that he had quietly and personally been urging a negotiated peace. "I can't say anything about this now," he confided, "and I don't want to be quoted publicly. Some day it will come out in my memoirs, and then people will be able to judge for themselves my position on this tragedy in Southeast Asia." He added that after our lunch he was meeting with Henry Kissinger, pressing him for immediate, productive steps to establish a peace settlement.

The next day Ralph Menconi and I flew to New York on the Eastern shuttle. As the plane circled and climbed over the nation's capital, I told Ralph, "Many of us have been unfair to Graham. He has been much more aware of his position as a world Christian leader than many of his critics realize. He knows that while his opponents can pop off and demand that he take a stand on this issue or that national policy, his being in touch with the top leadership requires a great deal of patience, persistence, and timing. It's also true that few of us are experts and Graham knows where to locate his expertise: that's when he's preaching from the Bible."

Ralph stared out the window as we lifted away from the Potomac basin. "Maybe that's why he has remained such a durable Christian leader," Ralph mused. "He knows when to speak and when to be silent."

The world sees the public ministry of Billy Graham and what do they observe? Success, continuity, growth, and popularity. But what is not in view, those things which do not appear, require our understanding and appreciation to gain a slant on his whole life. If one would look at the twenty-five years of his public exposure, statements, interviews, and media comments, we would be absolutely amazed to find such a thoughtful, reflective, and humble person.

In nearly three decades Graham has made perhaps two or three comments that have really angered his enemies and hurt his friends. Once was when he doubted that John Kennedy would be a strong President, especially with the Roman Catholic influence that surrounded his life. Norman Peale and Dan Poling shared this concern and went on to challenge Kennedy's bid for the presidency. Billy carefully extricated himself from that political potboiler, but he realized that his comments or endorsements of public figures was frightfully complicated. Since then he has resisted all invitations to support candidates or policies publicly. (During the Goldwater–Johnson campaign Billy received thousands of telegrams from Barry's followers pleading with him to publicly endorse the Republican candidate. He refused.)

The second major blunder that Billy made was his off-hand suggestion that rapists should be castrated. That was greeted with a general uproar some years ago when he made the remark on an overseas trip, and he quickly apologized for such a "thoughtless and insensitive suggestion." With the soaring increase in rape and personal abuse of victims, Billy undoubtedly felt a desperate need to find some means to control this violent sexual pattern of men in our society.

The temptation for Billy Graham to enter politics usually comes through the agency of friends who see him as a personality bringing respect, morality, and hope to the American public. Yet Billy realizes that this can never be his calling. He has intimated to advisor-friends that his closeness to the last several presidents

has revealed his fascination for the power and force of the office —
and the need for him to resist for himself this temptation to
power.

*It may be that Billy's greatest success as a person and largest
contribution to the United States during this past half century is
his determination to stay out of politics and to be removed from
swaying this fickle population one way or another.* Those like
myself who were dismayed at Graham's unqualified support of
the Johnson–Nixon policy in Vietnam may have neglected to
admit how restrained Billy was during this period of conflict. If
he had had the temperament and rage of some other religious
personalities, he surely would have been preaching an American
Holy War, using all his skills and the indulgent media at his
command. To have launched such a crusade would have been
hard to control and difficult to turn off.

Graham has never seen himself as a political "messiah," or
even, for that matter, some mighty prophet of the Lord. He is
simply an evangelist. He is introduced at all his Crusades as
simply "Mr. Graham." This is the most natural expression of his
humility — humility which, says U. S. Senator Mark O. Hatfield,
"is the most extraordinary quality of the man." Hatfield has
known Graham for more than twenty years. The two are close
spiritually and intellectually. Hatfield, you recall, was the person
Graham proposed to Nixon as his running mate in 1968. (Nixon
chose Spiro T. Agnew instead.)

In a world and society populated by "big people," with "large
egos" that require regular feeding and stroking, Graham is not to
be linked with such company or with such needs. His inner
prayer life and the goals that he established for himself reveal a
Christian without malice toward his critics or most vocal opponents — and a shining affection for the people whom God has
created.

When Ralph Looney, editor of the *Albuquerque Tribune,*
interviewed Graham during a Southwestern Crusade, he came
away shaking his head. This newspaper veteran of the Scripps–
Howard chain said, "I am absolutely amazed. I could never
expect to meet such a person as Billy Graham. His way is so direct

and personal. He is absolutely frank, never gave me an evasive or
cagey answer. He asked about *my* work and *our* city. We had a
rare, genuine exchange of ideas. I consider him a friend."

During the interview Graham revealed to Looney that he had
been in touch with former President Nixon and had offered
prayerful concern for his health and the well-being of Pat.
Looney's exclusive interview became headlines across the country, since Nixon had been in contact with few people. Why had
Graham given this information to Looney? "Well," said Billy, "he
was the only editor who asked the question." The candor, care-
fulness, and humility of Graham are the qualities that have sustained him for these tumultuous decades of public Christian
service.

If humility is the living hallmark of Billy Graham (and he would
quickly correct this and say that it is his dependence on the grace
and love of God, nothing else sustains him), then two principal
expressions of that humility became a winning strategy for his
almost boundless success: the inclusion of all Christian groups
and a cooperative spirit to all Christian leaders, whether or not
they agree with him; and the early recognition that segregation
and racism are unbiblical and anti-Christian. Graham reached
this judgment on race several years before the big push in civil
rights demonstrations and the later developments of Black Power
and Equal Rights. In 1951 he insisted that his Crusades be
interracial. The Klan types and the extreme conservatives raged
at his determination of racial equality. But Billy persisted, and his
personal evangelistic Team has been integrated for more than a
decade.

ONE DAY

That morning in Scottsdale revealed a side of Billy that had not
surfaced before: his willingness, even eagerness to talk about the
work of the "total Christian" in an unbelieving world. And how
paradoxical it was, that just when the mainline churches in
America had drawn back from social involvement to bind their
wounds from the contests of the sixties (civil rights demonstrations, war protests, death-of-God debates), Billy was tooling up

his organization for global missions and international expression.

During our discussion, Graham reflected on the incredible Crusade held in Korea during the summer of 1973. The evangelist had preached to the largest gathering of people in the history of Christianity! One million people sang and prayed and listened to the message of the American Christian. However, this joyous celebration, revealing such intense spiritual hunger, had its dark edges: the totalitarian regime of President Park.

For several years Park and his cabinet had become nervous, then suspicious of the vitality and surging power of the Christian Church in Korea. Park's oppressive measures against the press and the universities had been fought head-on by both Catholics and Protestants. Park was increasingly wary of large gatherings, demonstrations, and public assemblies. Was the American preacher fronting for a Christian resistance movement that was about to surface and overthrow his iron Eastern rule?

"It was not a happy situation," said Billy, as he kicked off his sneakers. "For most evenings during that week of meetings, Ruth would stay up late at our hotel, reading her Bible out loud in order to give Park's people something to think about and struggle through in long translations."

Not only was the Grahams' room wiretapped, but their automobile as well. Park was taking no chances. At the climactic session in Seoul, more than seven thousand police showed up to "direct traffic." Since only a few hundred cars arrived, it was apparent that the alarm was over crowds, not cars.

Today Billy is prepared to expend his energy and remaining active evangelistic days as a sparking force, an ignition point for Christians who want help at any point in the world.

As Billy was gearing up for major European Crusades of the summer of 1974 and 1975, he admitted that he was wrestling with the consequences of proposed visits in such diverse countries as Egypt and Italy. I had earlier reported to Billy my visit to Cairo in 1971 and my long afternoon discussion with a leading Moslem religious leader, Dr. Kamil Hussein, who had just retired as head of the University of Cairo Medical School. Dr. Hussein was in cordial and frequent conversations with Christians and a forceful advocate of Moslem–Christian dialogue.

As my host at several dinners, Dr. Hussein provided introductions to leading political and newspaper personalities. Yet I was startled by his questions to me concerning Billy Graham. Not Pope Paul or the Archbishop of Canterbury — but Billy Graham! He pointed out that Graham enjoyed a vast television audience in metropolitan Cairo (his broadcast beamed by Eurovision). This distinguished, educated Moslem leader considered Billy to be the best, most articulate speaker around. And Nasser hadn't been absent that long.

When I told Billy this, he responded by saying that his list of invitations included a strong request from the ecumenical community of Cairo (and certainly would have included Alexandria and its historic Christian institutions that are active at this moment) with the desire that a mass meeting be held on the shore of the Nile or some great sports stadium. Billy seemed hesitant, cautious, most reluctant to go.

"I'm not afraid for myself," Billy said, "although there is that element of danger in the turbulent Middle East with all of its blood-letting and instant violence. What concerns me is that such a Crusade in the United Arab Republic would cause thousands and thousands of Christians to be publicly identified with a white, Western, American evangelist. I would not want anyone to suffer needlessly for their loyalty to Christ and most certainly, never to be injured or abused by their appearance at one of our rallies."

(Graham went on to visit Greece and Belgium and Scotland that summer, but nothing developed from the Cairo invitation.)

There are many today who cherish the hope that Billy Graham will preach in Peking and Moscow before this century is over. And without too much praise and adulation it will be known as "his century" when they start to list the preachers of the ages. He is of the tradition of Wesley, Whitefield, Jonathan Edwards, and Charles Finney.

CHAPTER 6

Searching for the
Family of God

CHAPTER 6

Searching for the Family of God

"God does not die on the day when we cease to believe in a personal deity, but we die on the day when our lives cease to be illuminated by the steady radiance, renewed daily, of a wonder, the source of which is beyond all reason."

Dag Hammarskjold put these words in his journal, probably close to the era when the God-is-dead theologians operated so effortlessly in the slick magazines and on the television talk shows. We cannot imagine the burden Graham felt when so many apparently Christian professors and preachers slid off the deep end in this tank of theological sauce. Mainline church membership was in steep decline by the mid-sixties. The civil rights movement, rubbed raw by the convulsions of Vietnam, had finally been captured by a small group of radicals who demanded reparations from the established churches.

The incoherence of that period is marked by the uncertainty that shook denominational leaders to the core . . . how to respond carefully, openly, Christianly, to the irrational demands of intimidating radicals, especially those who were taunting the colleges, churches, and religious conventions. While some mainline churches wobbled and grew faint under the pressure, Graham showed a resoluteness and will that refused to accommodate the sophomoric behavior of such protests.

Historians will certainly note that during the wild and woolly period of the late sixties, the mainline churches went into sharp decline through their fuzzy response and uncertain moves that resulted from this head-on attack by non-Christian radicals. It will also be recorded that the larger Christian community remained firm, essentially through a conservative stance of cautious social outreach and a fierce will that the biblical witness of Christ's Church not be lost in the smoking excitement of barricade theology. Billy Graham was hammered from every side for his establishment, support-the-President stance regarding the Vietnam disaster; on civil rights, he continued to maintain his policy of no-integration-no-Crusade. This was not enough for the most militant players in the Southern Christian strategy. But it reflected the sentiment of the evangelist, and he kept to this policy no matter what the attack from radicals and liberals and reactionaries.

Some threatened to upset the Graham rallies, but they never lost a beat during this hour of controversy and confrontation. In one incident, individuals bent on disrupting and picketing a Graham meeting were simply surrounded and nudged out of the hall. Other incidents were minor. People may not have liked Billy's position, but they never doubted his willingness to enforce what he believed. Some campus critics argued that Billy's firm putdown of their behavior identified him as simply the chaplain of "law and order." Billy's response was direct, better than outlaw and disorder.

In a new book, *Understanding Tomorrow*, Lyle Schaller identifies much of the conflict — setting ground rules which had been laid in the early sixties and were to blow up in the face of the progressive wing of the Church. Billy had always shied away from the legislative answers, the secular resolutions that captivated so many willing people. Billy kept arguing for a change inside the person — the other branch of Christendom kept calling for a change in the landscape, a revision in the social, political, economic arrangement. Schaller concludes:

> The 1960's produced at least two important streams of thought that continue to influence the thinking of many people as they look toward tomorrow. One is the optimism of the Kennedy-Johnson era and operated on the assumption that if only good people would try harder, most of the injustices and inequities of American society could be erased. Out of this came the movement for a Great Society. . . . Caught up in this stream were the politicians, church leaders, social workers, businessmen, teachers, and foundation executives as well as leaders of minority groups.

Small wonder we had the street–campus rage five years later.

The editors of *The Wall Street Journal* would view this wreckage by observing, "The students who reject history and find thinking uncongenial are fools who will never understand the world or man, and they will suffer for it. Similarly, the militants who demand black academic separatism and disregard for academic standards are asking for a second-class education — if that — and they will suffer for it. . . . Part of the anti-intellectualism is an arrogant contempt for the rights of others. So we have college deans held prisoner, files rifled, precious manuscripts destroyed, church services disrupted by militants demanding financial reparations for Negroes. . . ."

Even today the new barbarians rattle the gates, demanding open admission policies to the university of many states, free tuition, passing grades for everyone, and instant professional placement upon graduation. Alas, the world is too wise and harsh for that; however, the Christian community has had its heavy share of advocates for such absurdity. While some of the smoke and uproar accompanied church leaders in their handling of such delicate matters, Graham represented for millions of Christians an unwavering standard — someone to be trusted and followed.

Following the debacle of the Angela Davis affair (in which certain Presbyterian leaders committed $10,000 in church mission funds as a grant for her defense "to insure that she would receive a fair trial"), Dr. Richard Knox Smith, United Presbyterian leader in the Southwest, concluded that his denomination isn't being led, it is merely responding. Responding to input from pressure groups and special interests; responding to headlines and responding to appeals and demonstrations. This is commonly called, "letting the world set our agenda."

Smith went on to argue that if the roar and muscle of the world continued to set the agenda for the Church, there wasn't going to be much left to spend or share. Membership was dropping, gifts were thinning out, and cash reserves were being exhausted in Great Society ventures draped in religious garb. . . . Graham and his people understood this inherently. They did not scold their progressive Protestant/Catholic brethren. They just let the consequences take their awful toll of social concern without personal salvation, community action without congregation support, policy statements without popular understanding.

Many in the intellectual-sophisticated ranks of the Christian Church have faulted Graham for a narrow social vision and a too-heavy concentration on the individual and what the individual person — soul — should be doing about finding a living relationship with Christ. For a quarter of a century the wise heads in leading seminaries and prominent college stations have mocked Graham for his revivalistic idolatry, his old-time pietism, his strong emphasis on prayer, Bible reading, and devotions with the family. To change the world, they argued, was to change Congress, to rework social structures, to manipulate mass media, and *this* was the essence of Christianity in the twentieth century. The self-development of people became a glistening slogan; salvation would come through process, through employment opportunities, through advocacy channels.

Some of this worked, and some people found love and justice and saluted the Church. But too often this was a self-illusioning process, for it denied the efficacy of the Holy Spirit and sublimated the meaning of conversion and regeneration.

By 1970–71 the swaying, slipping wreckage of so many bright social-improvement promises had come down, especially hard upon the churches. The conservative congregations flourished, and Graham's Crusades went on from strength to strength, almost a living judgment upon the mistaken, misguided yearnings of the liberal wing. In a way, Billy helped to hold the Christian community together while the National Council of Churches and the World Council of Churches slowly sank in an ocean of red ink. The dollar votes were being counted, and an era had come to an end.

Sometime during the past ten years Billy Graham became "acceptable" to almost every branch and description of the Christian life. A large part of that acceptance and belonging is a direct result of his support of missions overseas. While Billy has maintained Crusade Headquarters in Australia and temporary bases in Japan and Hong Kong, almost every country that has a viable Christian Church knows Graham to be supportive and helpful, not competitive and factious.

When you study the sponsor lists of churches and religious personalities in Scotland or Belgium or Brazil, you find a wide band of Christian cooperation behind Billy's scheduled appearances. This is because of an early, conscious decision on the evangelist's personal belief and operational strategy:

> They kept to their determination never to work in a city without an invitation from a substantial group of representative churches. . . . They moved from city to city with apparently inexhaustible energy, working four or five weeks in each. Wherever they went the Team left behind a host of friends and converts, and sometimes critics. Nevertheless, one of the most significant developments of the early nineteen fifties was the widening range of church support behind him.[1]

Billy moved easily in this broad spectrum of theological differences that have always caused unrest in the Christian community. One of his most recent invitations has been to preach in Poland, a journey that gained the approval of Pope Paul VI — with one suggestion: Take your own translator. In regard to the Catholic interest in Graham's present ministry, it is acknowledged by the Graham Team that the Vatican is most cordially supportive of the new invitation extended to Billy by the twenty-two Protestant churches of Rome. The social and political upheaval within Italy and the advancing secularity of Italian youth have brought these two groups to a mutual desire that the American preacher will ultimately hold a Crusade in the Holy City.

In one respect this is tantamount to admitting the ineffectiveness of the Catholic community in Italy to deal with its own spiritual decline. On the other hand, it reveals a fresh grasp of the powerful and essential meaning of Christian evangelism and Christian proclamation in a secular society. In the last analysis, Rome is asking for the man who is "number one" in the Christian front lines.

In several recent meetings in the Southwestern United States, Billy has continued to be impressed with the widespread growth of the Jesus People and the Jesus Freaks. Many of them have been showing up at Graham rallies. On a recent California visit, two young Jesus kids, complete with Levi cut-offs, long hair, and well-thumbed Bibles, wangled an interview with the evangelist from Montreat. At the very beginning of the interview one of them blurted, "Do we threaten you?" Graham laughed, "Threaten me! Listen, you're doing what I have been called to do for at least twenty-five years. You're a sign of success. You people are the confirmation of all that I have been about. You're the future — keep it up. God bless you."

That dashing, flashing young Baptist preacher from North Carolina, the whirlwind pastor with the Southern drawl and the natty suits of 1949, now looks like Mr. Straight to the new generation that is discovering him in their teen years. "Well," mused Billy, running his hands through his gray hair, "I'm no teen-ager. I am a fifty-seven-year-old grandfather, and I'm not going to wear sandals, tie-dyed shirts, and faded jeans. I'm going to keep being myself, and I believe that young people respect that. I certainly respect them, but I'm not caught up in their fads or style of dress. Many church members are getting a little tight over the tactics of the Jesus Generation. They can be rude and abrasive — yet most of them seem to be sincere, born-again Christians. Of course, like their elders, the Jesus movement is splitting into conservative-radical divisions and I suppose that's inevitable, with the Campus Crusade and Youth for Christ speaking to conservative kids and groups like the Post Americans, now the Sojourners, touching those who are very radical in their social viewpoint. But, you know, I can agree with 90 percent of what they have to say."

Billy is not a politician, but like a politician he has a canny, intense sensitivity to the trends and movements that are sweeping through our civilization. He was one of the earliest to see the arrival of the Jesus Freaks on the scene and later wrote a book about it called *The Jesus Generation*. This was a collection of fourteen sermons given in 1971 and addressed primarily to young people, identifying their problems and personal hangups.

Graham's preaching style and sermonic material follow the same pattern: he establishes his subject, either some current event or a Bible story, and then applies it to the question of drugs or sexual promiscuity or teen-age rebellion. His response to the theme is sound moral advice, emphasizing that all are sinners and must find forgiveness from God in Christ. He affirms the belief that Christ is the answer to their deepest need and that in belonging to Him is to belong to the central power of the universe.

One of the most interesting aspects of *The Jesus Generation* happens to be the introduction. In an autobiographical manner Billy tells of the time he was serving as the grand marshal of the Tournament of Roses Parade in Pasadena in 1971. He describes his emotions as he rode along in an open car, sensing not only the greatness of America but also its sickness and dying need for revival. He observed many young people along the parade route holding religious placards, carrying Bibles, and making the sign of the clenched fist with the index finger pointing upward and shouting religious slogans. Graham had an almost irresistible urge to get into the street and identify with them. Suddenly he was spontaneously returning the upward gesture, shouting "One Way — The Jesus Way!"

Graham offered an astute list of the qualities of the Jesus Movement in America and Europe as he came to know it:

1. The movement, thus far, centers in Jesus. It is spontaneous. No one leader has emerged.
2. The movement is Bible-based. They see the Bible as the "ir-

refutably accurate word of God . . . solving all their problems from the cosmic to the trivial. For them, as one father observes, it's the ultimate 'how-to' Book."[2]

3. There is a demand for an "experience" with the risen Christ. These young people expect more than an intellectual acceptance — you have to be with the living Christ.

4. These young people are putting a renewed emphasis on the power of the Holy Spirit. "Ten years ago I asked Dr. Karl Barth what the new emphasis in theology would be during the next twenty years. He replied without hesitation, 'The Holy Spirit.' Little did I dream it would come through a youth revival in America."

5. The Jesus generation is finding a cure for drugs and other vicious, self-destructive habits. "One of the great drug experts in America told me recently that the only certain cure for drug addiction he had found was a religious experience."

6. These young people are open and eager to Christian discipleship.

7. There is evidence of a keen social responsibility, touching persons of all races.

8. The Jesus kids obviously display an incredible zeal for evangelism.

9. The second coming of Christ has a receptive audience in the thinking and discussion of the Jesus Generation.

But in saying all this, Billy draws this conclusion regarding the young people of today, revealing his persistent interest in young people and his determination not to be swayed by isolated victories or sudden success at a specific Crusade:

I do not want to leave the impression that the majority of American young people are suddenly turning to Christ. . . . The vast majority of American young people are still alienated, uncommitted, and uninvolved. . . . It is to that alienated, rebellious, uncommitted majority that most of this book is directed — those who are enduring the "changing scene" and "bad vibrations."[3]

GRAHAM AS A SEARCHER

One of the most vivid memories I have of Billy Graham is not at a Crusade in some vast arena in the United States, but of his walking up, alone, to the front entrance of the enormous University center at Uppsala, Sweden, as a visitor to the meeting of the

World Council of Churches. It was in 1968, and thousands of delegates from around the world joined in this conclave.

Billy should have been a special guest, perhaps to address the convention on the meaning and purpose of evangelism. But ecclesiastical jealousies are so intense and long-standing, that the man from Montreat was there simply as an American visitor in sport coat and dark glasses, with a newspaper under his arm. He sat alone in the bleachers that surrounded the immense sports arena floor where official delegates were seated and deliberating. Billy had come to be a part, even at the distant edges, of this gathering of Protestants, Orthodox, and Roman Catholic official observers. While some of their leadership had in essence rejected him (they had invited Pope Paul — declined), he had not ruled them out, and there he was, interested and attentive. He had not only compassion but class.

We met later in a smaller meeting: Ken Wilson and I from the *Christian Herald*, Harold Lindsell from *Christianity Today*, David Hubbard from Fuller Seminary, and Billy Graham. The topic — "How to instill a greater spiritual awareness and urgency of bringing the gospel to the whole world." Some of those present were members of various voting blocs and saw opportunities to introduce the theme. Billy spent much of his time visiting with Christians from India on the plight of the Church in the subcontinent. But he came to participate, whether guest, delegate, or observer. His presence indicated a strength that has been one of his abiding secrets of a quarter-century of Christian preaching: Never shut anyone out. Include every Christian as part of your fellowship unless he or she excludes himself or herself (such as Dr. Carl McIntire and the more rabid fundamentalists or, for that matter, the more rabid liberals). Graham refuses to draw tight circles either in his ministry or his personal fellowship.

THE CAPACITY FOR GROWTH

"How I wish I could take back some of the statements made in those early days because of immaturity or lack of knowledge and experience. . . . I was woefully unprepared for this new responsibility. . . . I found myself addressing conventions and groups which demanded much more than I could give."[4]

This was Billy's response to his most constant critic, *The Christian Century.* He wrote this in an outstanding essay on his evangelistic ministry as part of a series being published by the Chicago-based journal called, "How My Mind Has Changed." The world's leading preachers, pastors, and theologians wrote for the series; Graham's article was sensational in candor and forthrightness.

Of the seven points in his essay, Graham admitted that he could not be an expert in everything; theology was not his big suit, but generosity in spirit could be everybody's goal. He recognized the need to *narrow* the limits of his evangelistic endeavor:

> The message of the evangelist is "narrow": It does not spread-eagle out into the broad ramifications of total theology or sociology. Contrary to the opinion of some, the evangelist is not primarily a social reformer, a temperance lecturer, or a moralizer. . . .
> He is simply a proclaimer of the good news.

In this four-thousand-word article, the evangelist noted that his concept of the Church had taken on a new dimension. "Ten years ago," he wrote, "my concept of the church tended to be narrow and provincial, but after a decade of intimate contact with Christians the world over I am now aware that the family of God contains people of various ethnological, cultural, class, and denominational differences. I have learned that there can be minor disagreements of theology, methods, and motives but that within the true church there is a mysterious unity that overrides all divisive factors. . . . Christians do not always agree, but they can disagree agreeably and that what is most needed in the church today is for us to show an unbelieving world that we love one another."

With that Graham wrote his work and his ministry into a whole new stage of religious endeavor.

In the early stages of his ministry, Graham received some regular and rigorous criticism from the theological heavyweights on the liberal side of Protestantism and Roman Catholicism. Reinhold Niebuhr came down from Mount Olympus from time to time to offer Graham suggestions to improve content and social application of the gospel. In a most sincere and disarming gesture, Billy later responded to the criticism through an interview in *The Saturday Evening Post:*

> When Dr. Niebuhr makes his criticisms of me, I study them for I have respect for him. I think he has helped me to apply Christianity to the social problems we face and has helped me to comprehend what those problems are. But I disagree with Dr. Niebuhr in one respect. I don't think you can change the world with all its lusts and hate and greed, until you change men's hearts. Men must love God before they can truly love their neighbors. The theologians don't seem to understand that fact. . . .[5]

If Billy has grown, it comes through his willingness to hear the critics, to weigh the judgments of friends as well as those opposed to him, study seriously the suggestions of those with whom he differs theologically. He will not yield on the centrality of the Scripture or the power of the Holy Spirit to change and convert lives, nor will he yield on the love and grace of God to rescue a sin-sick world. Those beliefs are absolute and unchangeable. But much about Billy and his Team has undergone significant and healthy alteration.

Billy painfully recalls an experience on the White House lawn early in his ministry. He and his Team knelt, right on the grass, wearing those big, beautiful hand-painted ties, loud sport coats, and white buck shoes. They were showing the Washington press photographers how they had just prayed with the President, Mr. Truman. (Small wonder that the man from Missouri did not attend Graham's public rally!) The scene was absolutely herky-jerky, with Billy's Southern you-all pack praying for the flashbulbs. The embarrassment of that day was a life-long learning-growing experience for Graham. He later refused to be pictured with Elvis Presley to avoid the showmanship, stuntman-ship label.

The real growth in Graham's personality and in his organization corporately came not from the superficial stunts with national leaders nor from the acquisition of more conservative suits and better grammar. Rather, it was found in the growing awareness of the worth of other Christians; it came through an appreciation that fundamentalists did not have all the answers and that liberal followers of Christ could make a loving and lasting witness in the world. (A dramatic example of such a conservative-liberal coalition came a century earlier, when Dwight L. Moody, evangelist, became acquainted and then a friend for life with Henry Drummond, Scottish scientist. Drummond's lecture and book, *The Greatest Thing in the World*, gained incredible popularity in the United States through the sponsorship of the Moody people and Dwight L. himself. The Moody-Drummond friendship created an important bridge between Christian camps that earlier had issued only polemical statements toward the faith and theology of the other.)

By the nature of the evangelists' business — reaching people — and the necessity of the evangelists' style — travel and contact with new societies and traditions among Christians — Graham moved steadily away from the rigidity and harshness of the far-right fundamentalists. In one sense, his own family as well as his wife's, the Nelson Bells, had seeded his perspective with a wide opportunity for cooperation and cordiality among Christians. Billy's parents had been Reformed Presbyterians; the Nelson Bells were Southern Presbyterians with a medical missionary investment in the Church of China. While Billy later — at college age — came into the orbit of the Southern Baptist Convention, he was under no compulsion to repudiate his Presbyterian heritage and was to regard Nelson Bell as a life-long spiritual counselor.

Graham's spiritual odyssey took him into a mosaic of worldwide religious friendships (as well as trust with a variety of Christian expressions in the twentieth century); but it also took him *away from* a restrictive theological climate that could well have crushed his career and ministry had he stayed under its influence. Carl F. H. Henry, first editor of *Christianity Today* and long-term Graham advisor, put that setting in sharp profile when he wrote,

> What distressed the growing evangelical mainstream about the fundamentalists' far right were its personal legalisms, suspicion of advanced education, disdain for biblical criticism per se, polemical orientation of theological discussion, judgmental attitudes toward those in ecumenically related denominations, and an uncrit-

ical political conservatism often defined as "Christian anti-communism" and "Christian capitalism."⁶

There are many within the world Christian community who believe that Billy failed them during the Vietnam crisis, especially because of his close personal identification with Lyndon Johnson and, later, Richard Nixon, both of whom kept pressing for victory in Southeast Asia. Historians from the sixties wince from the replay of the Graham tapes of that period, for they hear America's most prominent Christian spokesman linking Jesus Christ with the war policies of Lyndon Johnson. In 1966 President Johnson heard Billy say, in Texas, that Jesus told His followers, "I am come to send fire on the earth (Luke 12:49)." Then reading from Matthew 10:34–36: "Think not that I am come to send peace on earth; I came not to send peace, but a sword. For I am come to set a man at variance against his family. And a man's foes shall be those of his own family."

During this rally, Graham went on to state that "there are those who have tried to reduce Christ to the level of a genial and innocuous appeaser; but Jesus said, You are wrong — I have come as a fire-setter and a sword-wielder." This is and was accurate Scripture and sound New Testament preaching. What alarmed so many was the presence of a President who could only read this as a justification for further American military conflict in Southeast Asia. In full irony, the "fire and the sword" and the "division of household" all came back to collapse Johnson's administration and force him not to seek reelection. It also would haunt Richard Nixon in a variety of other scenes.

The majority of citizens in this country at that time would have applauded Graham's speech and implied endorsement of the Vietnam policy. But by 1970, at the celebration of Honor America Day on the Fourth of July, Billy revealed a deeper understanding of the plight and purpose of the American experiment in freedom. At this Nixon-sponsored, controlled, patriotic, flag-waving event, the evangelist introduced some strong and enduring reasons for honoring the fifty states. His first reason was the reality of America's invitation to the distressed and persecuted of the world — that here they could find freedom and independence. Graham also mentioned the generosity of Americans — reaching out to those suffering from famine, disease, or natural disasters wherever they may occur.

Then, just prior to Watergate, he noted that this open society has always been prepared to discuss its problems in front of the world. Poverty, racial conflict, and injustice are publicly debated, and the world is able to see an open forum. He said, "We honor America because she defends the right of her citizens to dissent. Dissent is impossible in many countries of the world, whereas constructive dissent is the hallmark of our freedom in America." Billy shuddered at disruptive and violent protest, yet he knew that dissent was at the core of the American democratic process. Vietnam had become a personal growth feature, and Billy carried its pain as he visited the front lines and later saw the casualties from both sides.

Although Billy would hold to his claim that the evangelist's ministry must have a "narrow" limit so as not to dilute or hinder the proclamation of the Good News, he came to acknowledge that "my belief in the social implications of the gospel has deepened and broadened. I am convinced that faith without works is dead. I have never felt that the accusations against me of having no social concern were valid. Often the message of the evangelist is so personal that his statements on social matters are forgotten or left out when reports are made. It is my conviction that even though evangelism is necessarily confined within narrow limits the evangelist must not hedge on social issues."

It is apparent that the heart of the problem for Christians and their friends is not whether or not a leader in the Church speaks out on social issues, but whether or not that voice is supportive of our stand and endorses *our* viewpoint. That will always be the crux of the debate and not the presence of a person like Graham in the public arena.

Ardent Christians and the most zealous advocates of the Word of God have consistently sensed the requirements that indicate the calling of God's people into strange and surprising areas. John Calvin, who established so much that is good and lasting and powerful in the Reformed tradition, not only brought the cutting edge of the Word of God to Geneva, Switzerland, but also saw the need to create schools, hire street sweepers, and recruit dentists. He believed these policies to be an extension of God's will.

When Adoniram Judson reached the interior of Burma with the gospel, he discovered another role as a Christian among an illiterate people — to give them a written language. From this civic and educational improvement, he added his skills in assisting Burmese to write trade agreements and perform duties akin to being secretary of state. In the same manner David Livingstone not only healed the bodies of sick Africans, but immediately showed them how to heal their sick crops and declining harvests by introducing irrigation to the land. He brought a message of hope that saved cities as well as souls.

Graham has moved to a position of seeing the whole gospel for the whole man. And out of this perspective has come his unyielding policy of unsegregated services in the South and his challenging of apartheid policies in South Africa. All the liberal rhetoric in Western civilization did not accomplish what his Crusade attained in Durban, South Africa, when he addressed 45,000 people in King's Park Rugby Stadium in 1973. It was the first and largest nonsegregated gathering in the history of the country. It was an answer to Billy's prayer — and a sign of his life-long commitment to the belief that at the foot of the cross the ground is level.

Billy and the Bible

Billy and the Bible

"All the world's answers are right in this little book."
— Billy Graham pointing to his pulpit Bible

In the spring of 1976 *Catholic World* published an extensive interview with Billy Graham. The reporter asked personal, probing questions about Billy's ministry, the state of the Christian Church around the world, and the evangelist's appeal to Roman Catholics. To a statement about the power and strength that flowed from the preacher's message, Graham replied,

> I am giving what the Bible says and the Word of God has its own built-in power to penetrate the human heart.

Then writer Ed Wakin asked,

> Why are you such a successful instrument of the Word of God?

Answer:

> Well, very much like Jonah, for example, or any of the prophets, the Word of the Lord came to me and I went out and taught. I believe the word of the Lord came unto me. He *called* me about thirty-five years ago to go out and proclaim the gospel.

This exchange between a Catholic writer and a popular evangelist reveals the source and center of Graham's success as a world figure — he has never strayed from the Bible, albeit at times offering a very literal interpretation of the Old and New Testament. Also, his response to the questioner reveals the translation of the Bible he prefers — the King James. Early in his ministry Billy acknowledged this preference for the King James Version, but he allowed that he read the Phillips paraphrase as well. His friends in the conservative Christian tradition have been caught up in the newer translations, which continue to present the Scriptures as the all-time best seller.

It was natural for Billy to slip into King James wording when replying to the interview question and to say, "The Lord came unto me." The first absolute of his public ministry, resolved in the early months of his preaching, was to believe everything *in* the Bible and not be concerned for what others thought *about* the Bible. This resolution gave Billy a consistent authority, and he has been unwavering in that commitment to a literal interpretation of Scripture.

That determination has affected thousands of listeners. One Princeton preacher said,

> I wouldn't know how to preach like Graham. For twenty years now I have been engaged, like most of our so-called modern preachers, in inventing logic, parable, intellectual forensics, and everything but the words of the Bible to prove that they are not wrong. Here comes this fellow who says the Bible is right because he believes in God; the Scripture are God's words. That's simply it. No need to fiddle around with any more proof than that.[1]

Most of Billy's theological confrontation comes from his literal interpretation of the Scriptures. (He once said that "hell is a literal place, not unlike Los Angeles.") This commitment arises from his trust in God's Word, since

> I am, in comparison with the great scholars of today, certainly uneducated. I came from a farm in North Carolina and never went to seminary or theological college. I did my work in anthropology and never went beyond an A.B. degree.

Many Christians appreciate and applaud Billy's ministry, and many mainline scholars such as John Mackay of Princeton have supported Graham's outreach to the lost and wandering masses.

By keeping close to the Bible, Billy has stayed next to a world view that does not perish with the changing of governments, cultures, or empires and is not swayed by fads or popular fancies. When critics worry about the "lasting effect" on the people who attend his Crusades, Billy says with biblical authority:

> I'm not the slightest bit concerned about it because I know the answer. I know that the parable of the sower in the thirteenth chapter of Matthew can be applied to every audience where the gospel is preached either by me or the simplest priest or clergyman in the world. There will be the person who will totally reject for "the seed falls on hard ground." There will be those where it will last maybe a month or two and fall by the wayside: "the thorns and the thistles will choke it out and the cares of the world may come in." But then there's the group where Jesus said, "They will believe and they will bear fruit sixty-fold and hundred-fold."[2]

Billy is living in the Bible as well as preaching from it.

When the reporter for *Catholic World* asked Billy if he had hope in a world so packed with trouble, he responded by saying,

> I have total hope. I was in the Senate dining room some time ago and Senator [Warren] Magnuson from Washington called me over to his table and said, "Billy, we're having an argument here on optimism and pessimism. Which are you?" I said, "I'm an optimist." He said "What makes you an optimist?" I said, "I've read the last page of the Bible. It's all going to come out all right. Utopia is going to come direct."[3]

The hopefulness (the term preferred by New Testament writers) that Billy teaches is a powerful and attractive force in everyone's life. Noted the evangelist:

> We are going to have Utopia. The Bible is full of it. The Bible teaches that Jesus Christ is going to come back again the second time. All the creeds of the Church teach it. The Church believes it, whether it teaches it or not. And the Bible has a tremendous program for the future that God has outlined. God's not going to leave us dangling; He's not going to let us blow ourselves into oblivion and destruction. God has a plan and yet we don't study it, we don't preach it. The average Christian today is totally ignorant of that book.[4]

Graham is probably responsible for more people buying the Bible than anyone else in this century. He wants his listeners not only going back to the Bible but living in the Bible for the future. His Crusades are saturated with the request, plea, even demand that new followers of Christ study and pursue the New Testament life. Frequently Billy uses literary techniques to summarize the Scriptures for those exposed to them for the first time in one of his mass meetings.

> The message of Jesus Christ, our Savior, is the story of the Bible — it is the story of salvation. Profound students of the Bible have traced the story of Jesus Christ from the beginning of the Old Testament, for He is the true theme of the Old as well as the New Testament.
>
> He appears in Genesis as the Seed of the Woman.
> In Exodus, He is the Passover Lamb.
> In Leviticus, He is the Atoning Sacrifice.
> In Numbers, He is the Smitten Rock.
> In Deuteronomy, He is the Prophet.
> In Joshua, He is the Captain of the Lord's Hosts.
> In Judges, He is the Deliverer.
> In Ruth, He is the Heavenly Kinsman.
> In the six books of Kings, He is the Promised King.
> In Nehemiah, He is the Restorer of the nation.
> In Esther, He is the Advocate.
> In Job, He is my Redeemer.
> In Psalms, He is my All in All.
> In Proverbs, He is my Pattern.
> In Ecclesiastes, He is my Goal.
> In the Song of Solomon, He is my Satisfier.
> In the Prophets, He is the Coming Prince of Peace.
> In the Gospels, He is Christ coming to seek and to save.
> In Acts, He is Christ risen.
> In the Epistles, He is Christ at the Father's right hand.
> In the Revelation, He is Christ returning and reigning.
> This is the eternal message of the Bible. It is the story of life, peace, eternity, and heaven. The Bible has no hidden purpose. It has no need for special interpretation. It has a single, clear, bold message for every living being — the message of Christ and His offer of peace with God.[5]

The Bible has become the driving force of Graham's Crusades, the cornerstone of his successful ministry, and the vocabulary of his life. If biblical truth sounds awkward, contradictory, or strange to modern man, that is the world's problem, not Billy's.

> As a Christian, I am under no obligation to attempt to reconcile the Bible's teachings with modern philosophy. . . .
> Biblical truth does not parallel human opinion of any generation; it usually opposes it! We are to be witnesses, not imitators. The prophets who spoke to their generations for God did not please or conform; they irritated and opposed.[6]

The vital core of Graham's preaching begins with the Bible's affirmation that God is the Creator of the universe, the world, and everything in it. The Old and New Testaments present man in rebellion against God — the act of people preferring themselves to God and His ways. In this break from divine law and God's plan, men found big trouble. Selfhood and selfishness produced civilizations saturated with lust, crime, war, greed, and racial hatred. Out of touch with their Creator, they came to war with each other.

After Billy reconstructs this biblical theme, he invariably draws his audience together by saying:

> The Bible reveals that in spite of man's rebellion God loves him. Thus God undertook the most dramatic rescue operation in cosmic history. He determined to save the human race from self-destruction, and He sent His Son Jesus Christ to salvage and redeem them. The work of man's redemption was accomplished at the cross.[7]

These two paragraphs reveal not only the heart of Billy's preaching but also provide the framework around which all Christians have been able to have fellowship and belonging. (Most differences that separate Christian bodies today and in the past have been over the style of church government, not convictions or doctrine about God's saving grace revealed in Jesus Christ.)

When Christians affirm their faith in Christ, they find that at least a spiritual unity and oneness has made possible the incredible success of the Graham Crusades. Billy does not come as one promoting a particular denomination — not many in England or Scotland were prepared to leave the Church of England or the

Presbyterian Church in Scotland for the Southern Baptist Convention! As he said to those 70,000 who thronged Wembley Stadium in London, in a chilling rain,

> This is the work of God, not Billy Graham. I have come here again to preach the same message I preached in Harringay. I have come to give you the Bible warning that you must be born again or you will never see the Kingdom of Heaven. I have come to say that unless ye be converted ye shall likewise perish [note the injection of King James biblical phrasing]. I am determined to know nothing among you save Jesus Christ and Him crucified [a direct quote from Paul].[8]

Billy was successful because he put his argument upon Scripture and his faith in Jesus Christ. Over and over again one discovers that people converted through his evangelistic ministry invariably point to this insistence that Scripture is the final authority and God is most fully revealed in the life and death and resurrection of His Son. Dr. David Rowlands, a British physician converted at a Graham rally in England, noted,

> Out of curiosity I went to hear Billy Graham. The message he preached was quite new to me. He kept repeating what God says in the Bible; I had been used to sermons based on rational arguments. I found his sermons heart-searching and disturbing, realizing for the first time in my life that I was a sinner, that my sins separated me from God: the sins of self, of lust, of materialism. These were my gods and the Bible teaches, "Thou shall have no other gods before me." I had broken the first commandment. I was a sinner needing a Savior.[9]

Billy makes powerful use of those biblical passages that point to man's impending doom unless he "turns and is saved." Employing the most powerful emotion — fear — has frequently been a source of criticism of Graham's preaching style. He has answered this charge in several ways — recognizing that he *does* use the element of dread, fear, and warning in his proclamation.

1. In a sermon in his New York Crusade of 1957, he stated,

> Many people say they do not believe that fear is a legitimate motive for coming to God. I disagree. I teach my children up on the mountain where we live to beware of rattlesnakes, lest they be bitten and die. This is legitimate fear. You teach your children to

watch out on the busy streets of New York lest they run out and be killed by a passing motor car. This is a legitimate fear.[10]

2. In one of his books Graham broached this topic by noting that in 1860, the French scientist Berthelot had been quoted as saying,

Within a hundred years of physical and chemical science, man will know what the atom is. It is my belief when science reaches this stage, God will come down to earth with His big ring of keys and will say to humanity, "Gentlemen, it is closing time!"[11]

Graham went on to point out how much of our daily life is saturated by secular publications that herald doom and destruction. He noted these titles reviewed by Michael Amerine in *The New York Times Book Review* as being current and factual:

> *Must We Hide?*
> *There Will Be No Time*
> *Manual for Survival*
> *Fear*
> *War and the Bomb*
> *Must Destruction Be Our Destiny?*
> *After Doom, What?*
> *Little World, Goodbye*[12]

Graham steadily points to the warnings and signs of trouble to come that Jesus shared with His disciples. We cannot do less. Our difficulty centers around our ignorance of the Bible and the truths of the gospel. Graham presumes that his audience is ignorant of the Old and New Testaments and needful of quick, precise summaries of Scripture. To recognize the arrival of the Savior, one of his summaries condenses the Old Testament in this manner:

> He would be of the tribe of Judah (Gen. 49:9,10)
> He would be born in Bethlehem (Mic. 5:2)
> He would be born of a virgin (Isa. 7:14)
> He would be called out of Egypt (Hos. 11:1)
> He would come as a prophet (Deut. 18:18,19)
> His own people would reject Him (Isa. 53:3)
> He would make a triumphal entry into Jerusalem (Zech. 9:9)
> He would be betrayed and sold for thirty pieces of silver (Zech. 11:12,13)

He would be put to death by crucifixion (Ps. 22)
His hands and feet would be pierced (Ps. 22:16)
Soldiers would cast lots for his clothing (Ps. 22:18)
He would be raised from the dead (Ps. 16:9,10)
He would ascend into heaven (Ps. 68:18)

ILLUSTRATIONS AND EXAMPLES

Any preacher of strength and persuasion must not only be familiar with the Bible, but bring a wealth of illustrations and examples from human experience as well. Poring over Billy's sermons and reading his books, one discovers that this speaker has a knack for the pithy quotation, the surprising story, and the clinching illustration. Graham has spent his intellectual life seeking out fresh encounters and interpreting these daily experiences as vehicles for revealing the truth of God in Christ.

Not until I undertook to write this book did I realize the vast range of the evangelist's story reserve, sustained by an almost insatiable search for new reflections of truth in the lives of people and human events. *Graham is an illustration genius.* Most people have not recognized or even acknowledged this skill in the evangelist. Critics are generally harping about the financial expenditures entailed in films, publications, and Crusades ("The money ought to be given to the poor" is the usual complaint) or dollars paid to this vast organization and operation. And if the megadollar annoyance is not mentioned, then some aspects of Graham's theology or a recent friendship with a President or a statement about a pressing social question is the source of debate. But no one, friend or critic, has underlined the amazing, ingenious technique that Graham has developed in regard to the illustrations which mark his preaching and writing.

The other aspect of this discovery is the fact that everything becomes published: through televised Crusades, *Decision* magazine, and daily newspaper columns. Consequently Graham cannot repeat himself. He must develop fresh material every day. (Several years ago he stated that his column was researched by staff in Minneapolis, but that he worked over every response personally and the final result "was my own.")

All librarians and researchers in the world cannot replace the sense of timing, incorporation, and interpretation that Billy puts into his mountain of material presented to the reading, listening, and viewing public.

Ten years ago *World Aflame* became a best seller. More than half a million copies were sold, yet the book never reached the recognition that it deserved beyond the Crusade audiences. The secret of *World Aflame* is the blend of Bible truths and hundreds of illustrations. Graham began:

> At 5:30 A.M. on July 16, 1945, a light brighter than a thousand suns illuminated the desert sands of New Mexico. One scientist who was watching wept. "My God," he exclaimed, "we have created hell." From that day on our world has not been the same. We have entered a new era of history — perhaps the last.[13]

That is a classic example of the Graham method — and theology. An event known and shared by people is retold with power and persuasion. A shared truth is highlighted, followed by Billy's pursuit of the theme of life's uncertainty, its possible and immediate end — and the saving, caring power of God in Christ for those who want to avoid hell now and hell later.

Graham generally attacks the presumptions and assurance of worldly figures, human institutions, and man's self-sufficiency which leads to arrogance and death. *World Aflame* took on the economists, the diplomats, and the educators. As for the latter, he pressed this example in his sermon:

> It is the assumption of some educators that the cause of world tension lies in the lack of knowledge and that if we can only educate every man, peace will come to the world. They say that if man knows better, he will do better. In *The Suicide of the West* which purports to explain the meaning and destiny of liberalism, James Burnham says that this plea of the educator overlooks entirely certain facts — that Germany, long one of the cultured nations of the world, produced a Hitler and a Himmler and that Joseph Goebbels had a Doctor of Philosophy degree. Burnham contends that highly educated people have inward drives, greeds, compulsions, passions, and a lust for power that are not eliminated by any known process of education.[14]

Billy likes to build the attention and tension of his point by using the experience of contrasting cultures and civilizations. When addressing the 1500 members of the Phoenix Executive Club in 1973, he pivoted around the theme of moral collapse in Western civilization and the need for America to return to its moral and spiritual roots. He illustrated his remarks by quoting James Reston of *The New York Times*, who had identified the atheists in charge of China as keenly committed to the virtues of work, honesty, and integrity. Quoting Chairman Mao, Graham pointed to the eight values (researched by Reston) worthy of reconsideration in the West: speak politely, pay fairly for what you damage, repay fairly, do not hit or swear at people, do not damage crops, do not take liberties with women, and do not mistreat captives.

During the tumultuous youth protests of the sixties, Graham associated himself with the yearnings of youth for change and creative revolution. But he warned of the excesses which can develop and destroy when youth goes wild with new power and becomes almost mad in the process. He recalled the youth crusades of the thirteenth century, particularly the one led by Stephen, a French shepherd who desired to liberate the Holy Land. Visions were reported and marvelous divine instruction revealed. Thousands flocked to the child-evangelist program, leaving home and family and destined to support God's work. Said Billy:

When Stephen's army of 30,000 children reached Marseilles, they rushed to the sea to watch its waters divide. Nothing happened. The promised miracle was a hoax. Hungry and maddened the youngsters spread through the city like wolves, pillaging, looting, and mugging.

Finally, two local merchants herded them into seven companies and promised to ship them to the Holy Land. Embarking on seven vessels, the fleet set out. Silence followed, and more years of silence.

Eighteen summers passed, and finally a priest who had accompanied them returned to tell his story. Two of the ships had been wrecked, losing all hands. The five remaining vessels had sailed on to Algerian and Egyptian ports where the children were handed over to waiting slave traders. The good-hearted merchants of Marseilles had been decoys. Sold into slavery and dispersed all over the Saracen Empire, the children were never heard from again.[15]

Although conservative in religious ideals, Billy was prepared to reach beyond the caution of his own generation in finding praise and appreciation for the bright ideas he saw emerging in the young people around him. His most effective point was always to cast his ideas in an autobiographical style:

> Soon after I was converted, I left the farm in North Carolina and went to school in Florida and later went to college near Chicago. At the end of World War II, I joined Youth for Christ International as their first full-time evangelist. When I went home to see my folks on the farm in North Carolina, I probably appeared "far out." I was smartly dressed, and my outfit included a colorful, hand-painted bow tie. My attire was certainly not conventional clerical garb, and I am sure my family was rather embarrassed to see me stand in the pulpit in such clothes.
>
> The younger generation doesn't want to be a rubber stamp of its elders. "A chip off the old block" is a phrase which would not appear in a youth dictionary.
>
> In the past we have required our young to defer significant feats both great and small, to be content with contests for grades and athletic letters, and to keep their heads buried in their books. So the average student, full-grown and exploding with energy, remains a dependent whose actions are monitored and whose life is carefully protected by his elders. As the years pass he grows increasingly restive, knowing himself to be an adult with a large stock of relevant knowledge, though with less experience than his parents, but often treated like a child. Today his universal rejection of this role is exploited by the radicals who have founded "the movement." It is international in scope, and it is passionate in commitment.
>
> But here is another side to the coin. Many times young people reject their parents for no reason at all. Many parents have done a good job rearing their children. Showering their children with love, they have spent hours every week with them. They have prayed earnestly for them and sacrificed much for them. Then when their children reach a certain age, they reject their parents. As Erich Segal put it, "I would define a father as a person who will someday be misunderstood by his son." One of life's most painful experiences is for a parent to be rejected by his child. This is happening more and more in our society. Often it is not the parent's fault — it is the child's fault. There is a certain indefinable age in the early teens at which God treats a child as an adult. Then

he must make his own moral decisions.

In concluding this chapter, I am going to say something which many of the older generation will not agree with, but which I have felt for a long time. Charles Reich is right in *The Greening of America*, and Bob Dylan, the Beatles, and the Birds in their lyrics, when they refer to a world being raped, robbed, and ripped off in a manner which litters our countrysides and renders our cities ugly and in parts uninhabitable. They point out the kind of treadmill, threadbare, plastic lives which too many millions of people are living in order to hang in there: in the business rat race; in keeping up with the Joneses socially or the brainheads intellectually. Life is much more than a tussle to come out top dog.[16]

If Graham is a storyteller, he is most effective when revealing spiritual truth through the agency of a humorous anecdote or event. Frequently this happens at the beginning of a sermon or talk, employing an "I'm O.K., you're O.K." technique with his audience:

> A few years ago a medical school graduate who had just obtained his M.D. degree began practice in a small village. An old man was his first patient. The young doctor was nervous about trying to make a good first impression. The old man listed all his ailments and waited for the doctor to give him a diagnosis. After a long examination, the young doctor had no clue as to what was wrong with his patient. Finally he asked: "Have you ever had this trouble before?" The old man said: "Yes, many times." The doctor said: "Well, you have it again." As we look at the distress, frustration, confusion, and deep maladies of our age, about all we can say is "The world has it again." But what does it have?[17]

Sometimes the preacher will inject a funny story or an absurd incident in the body of a message or sermon to illustrate some aspect of theology or teaching which may be getting heavy or complicated for the audience. When talking about the development of a personal faith, Graham insists that it must be accompanied by conscious acts of will. Faith without works is dead. So he remembers:

> I heard about a man some years ago who was rolling a wheelbarrow back and forth across Niagara River on a tightrope. Thousands of people were shouting him on. He put a two-hundred-pound sack of dirt in the wheelbarrow and rolled it over, and then he rolled it back. Then he turned to the crowd and said, "How many of you

believe that I can roll a man across?"

Everybody shouted! One man in the front row was very excited in his professed belief. The man pointed to this excited professor and said, "You're next!"

You couldn't see that man for dust! He actually didn't believe it. He said he believed it, he thought he believed it — but he was not willing to get in the wheelbarrow.

Just so with Christ. There are many people that say they believe on Him, they say they follow Him. But they never have gotten into the wheelbarrow. They actually never have committed and surrendered themselves wholly, one hundred percent to Christ.[18]

In a sermon on the new birth and what it means to be converted, Billy did an unusual switch by closing his talk with this amusing anecdote. Most clergymen would not dare to end a service on such an amusing story. Yet Billy would reply that his meetings first of all are a public happening, not a church service; and secondly, anything that clinches a new idea or motivation for a convert is proper for the preacher. So he said:

In Texas they tell a story about a man who used to hitch his horse every morning in front of the saloon. One morning the saloon-keeper came out and found the horse was hitched in front of the Methodist Church. He saw the man walking down the street and called out, "Say, why is your horse hitched in front of the Methodist Church this morning?"

The man turned around and said, "Well, last night I was converted in the revival meeting, and I've changed hitching posts."

That's what it means to be born again. That's what it means to be converted. It means that you change hitching posts.[19]

A Classic Graham Sermon

A Classic Graham Sermon

HOW TO TURN ABOUT . . .

AND HOW TO RELEASE FROM WITHIN YOURSELF

THE POWER OF THE IRRESISTIBLE GOD

Let us turn to the eighteenth chapter of Matthew's gospel and the third verse. We will start at the first verse.

> At the same time came the disciples unto Jesus, saying, Who is the greatest in the kingdom of heaven?
> And Jesus called a little child unto him, and set him in the midst of them.
> And said, Verily I say unto you, Except ye be converted, and become as little children, ye shall not enter into the kingdom of heaven.

What about this word *conversion?* The disciples came to Jesus and said, "Who is going to be first in Your kingdom?" Jesus had already said, "He that will be first must be last."

The requirement for entrance into heaven is true humility, not a false piety, but a true, genuine humility! It is the requirement that recognizes our need and our sin and the greatness and the majesty of God, and shows a willingness to receive Christ as Savior.

So, to illustrate the point, Jesus called a little child to Him and said, "Look at this little child, how trusting this little child is, how humble this child is." Before you can get to heaven you will have to become converted like a little child.

You must go back almost to your childhood, said Jesus. You must trust in God with the same simplicity, that same humility, that same dependence that a little child has for his parents.

In other words, conversion is simply a change in the direction of your life to a totally different direction.

That is the simple meaning of conversion. It means to turn around. It means to change.

A Chicago psychologist once said, "This generation needs converting more than any generation in history."

A famous British psychologist recently said, "We are so psychologically constituted as to need converting, and if the church fails to convert people, we psychologists are going to have to do it." So even psychology is recognizing the need for man to be converted.

The Bible teaches that you must be converted to enter heaven. The psychiatrist teaches that you must be converted in order to get the most out of life.

The question I want to ask is, Have you been converted to Jesus Christ? Do you know it, are you sure of it? If not, it could happen to you right now.

Conversion is taught all the way through the Bible. Ezekiel 36:26 says this: "A new heart also will I give you, and a new spirit will I put within you: and I will take away the stony heart out of your flesh, and I will give you an heart of flesh."

God is saying through Ezekiel, "I can give you a new heart."

Now, the "heart" all the way through the Scriptures stands for the seat of the soul — your ego, your intelligence, the seat of your emotions is said to be in the heart.

God says, "I'll take out the old heart and put in a new heart." God never patches anybody up. He never does it partially. He always performs a complete process of regeneration.

And conversion means you get a new nature; you get a new heart. Have you received a new nature?

In the gospel, Jesus calls conversion "being born again," "repenting of sin," "entering a narrow gate," and many other expressions.

Call it anything you like. Call it dedication. Call it surrender. Call it repentance. Call it grace. Call it anything you like.

Have you had this encounter with Christ? Peter calls it in Acts "repenting and being converted." Paul speaks of it in Romans as being "alive from the dead."

Second Corinthians 5:17 says: "If any man be in Christ, he is a new creature: old things are passed away; behold, all things are become new."

In Ephesians, Paul speaks of it as "quickening," or being made alive from the dead. In Colossians, Paul calls it a "[putting] off the old man with his deeds; and [putting] on the new man, which is renewed in knowledge after the image of him that created him."

In Titus, he calls it "the washing of regeneration, and renewing of the Holy Ghost."

In 2 Peter, the apostle says that we are made "partakers of the divine nature." In the First Epistle of John he calls it a passing "from death unto life."

If you pick up a Church of England Catechism it reads this way: "A death unto sin and a new birth unto righteousness."

The Bible teaches it, the church teaches it: you must be converted for the forgiveness of your sins.

The Bible says, "All of us have sinned." You might not have done all the sins in the book but you are a sinner, and I am a sinner. We have all come short of the glory of God. We have all failed to meet God's moral requirements.

Everyone of us has told a lie sometime, somewhere. Every one of us has had lust in our hearts, sometime, somewhere.

We have sinned against God, and this sin has come between us and God and this sin causes death — physical death, spiritual

death, and eternal death. That means separation from God —
judgment and hell.

Now, the greatest thing in life is to find forgiveness of sin. We
have only a few years here.

The Bible says that "our lives are spent as a tale that is told."

The Bible says that our lives pass quicker than a weaver's
shuttle.

The Bible says that life is only a shadow.

The Bible says that it is like the flower: it blooms and fades.

Our life passes so quickly that it is soon gone. God gives us a few
days, a few months, a few years, to find one thing, and that is
reconciliation to Him and forgiveness. God's forgiveness is the
greatest thing in life — worth more than a billion dollars. It is
worth more than a business empire. It is worth more than a
glamorous career. It is worth more than an education. It is worth
more than anything.

To be forgiven of sin! God says the only way that you can be
forgiven your sins and escape the judgment of hell is to be
converted!

Secondly, you need to be converted for your acceptance by
God. Because, you see, just as you are now, God cannot accept
you. Why, with your present evil nature, if you went to heaven, it
would be hell to you.

Suppose you went to heaven as you are. You don't enjoy a
prayer service down here on earth, you don't even enjoy a church
service, you go because it is a duty — something you have always
done.

It is traditional, but you do not particularly like to go to church.
You do not particularly like to be with God's people; you do not
like to read the Bible; you do not like to worship God.

Why, you would be miserable in heaven because that is all they
are going to do up there.

They will be worshiping God day and night, and if you could
not stand that for an hour down here, you would be squirming,
you would surely be in hell after the first three or four hours of
being in heaven.

So you don't want to go to heaven with your present nature.

You see, with your present nature, not changed by the power of Christ, you would be out of place up there.

Now you are a sinner, you have offended God. The Bible speaks of us as enemies of God. We have broken the laws of God. We deserve judgment and we are going to get judgment.

Somebody said, "But all I'm asking for is justice." No, I am not asking for justice, because if I were to get justice, I would be lost. I am not asking for justice; I want God's mercy.

And I see it in Jesus Christ's death on the cross, when He shed His blood for my sins. I see in His death the love of God, the mercy of God, the grace of God extended toward me. And when I come and, by faith, receive His Son, I am said to be converted and changed and God comes into my life.

A new life begins. I have become a partaker of the divine nature, and in that moment I am said to be justified — just as if I had never sinned.

In other words, God does not only forgive us, He places us in a position higher than Adam before he sinned. We are placed in God's sight as though we had never committed a sin, so that God even forgets our sin.

We need to be converted for entrance into heaven. Jesus said, "Except ye be converted and become as little children, ye shall not enter into the kingdom of heaven."

I did not say it; Jesus said it. Do you think Jesus was lying? You haven't been converted? Then you will not get to heaven. That is what Jesus said.

You say, "Oh, we will make it somehow, for God is a wonderful God. He is a God of love and He is a God of mercy. Certainly He is going to get us there."

Yes, He is a God of mercy, He is a God of love, not willing that any should perish but that all should come to repentance.

But if you go on rejecting Christ and go on without conversion to Him, there is nothing God can do about it, because you sin away the mercy and the grace of God and there remains nothing but judgment to come.

God is not only mercy, not only love and grace; God is judgment. And the wrath of God shall be poured out upon men who are outside of Christ. Would you enter heaven today? Suppose you dropped dead right where you are, would you enter the kingdom of heaven? Are you sure? How many of you know that you will be alive tomorrow? Are you willing to gamble the next twenty-four hours, to gamble on the fact that you will live?

I believe everyone is counting on being in heaven. You are counting on being saved. You are counting on being received by God into heaven. Yet, you have not even done what God said are the basic requirements of entrance into the kingdom.

Jesus said that no one will enter the kingdom who has not been converted.

You say, "Well, Billy, what is involved in conversion?" Well, first there must be repentance. What does repentance mean?

Repentance means to change your mind, to change your feelings, to change your purpose, to change your conduct.

It is intellectual, it is emotional, it is volitional.

It means that I look at my sins and I'm willing to say to God, "I am a sinner."

I talked to a man one day, and before I could get a word in edgewise he was telling me how good he was, how much he had given away, what he was doing for other people.

All of that is fine, but that does not merit your salvation.

The Bible says that all our righteousness is as filthy rags in the sight of God.

You can obey the Golden Rule and still not be in the kingdom of God.

Nicodemus was as fine a Pharisee as ever lived. He kept the law, but Jesus said, "Nicodemus, you need to be born again."

A rich young ruler had kept all the commandments, but Jesus said, "If you want to enter heaven, one thing you lack — you must admit that you are not fully committed to God. Your love of money stands in the way."

Are you willing to admit that?

Intellectually you must say, "I am a sinner."

Recognize you are a sinner, and if you ever get a vision of God — who He is and what He is — you will in all humility say, "O God, I am a sinner."

Do you know how God compares you?

He does not compare you with other people. You may be better than 90 percent of the people in America.

God compares you to Jesus. He compares you with His Son. And there is not a person here who can stand up and say, "I'm as good as Jesus."

If you come short of Jesus, you are a sinner. You must recognize that. You must acknowledge it, and then there is a change of feeling.

You know, it's a strange thing today that people don't want any emotion in religion. I never tell a deathbed story. I never tell a story to try to work on people emotionally. I think that is wrong.

I think that it is deceitful on the part of the evangelist or the preacher to work deliberately on the emotions of people. Having said that, I agree with Dr. W. E. Sangster, the great Methodist preacher of London.

Dr. Sangster said some time ago, "Anybody that will go to a football game and shout, and anybody that will go to a baseball game and yell 'kill the umpire,' and then say you should never have any emotion in religion, that man does not deserve any attention whatsoever."

Isn't it a strange thing that we can sit in front of a television set and bite our fingernails off watching "Bonanza," or when the baseball game is on we watch the World Series with all our emotions running wild, and in the background people are shouting.

But in church, if you shed a tear, or even smile or have any emotion or any feeling, you are suspect immediately.

No wonder Dr. John MacKay, the former president of Princeton Theological Seminary, speaking to the students on the opening day of school a few years ago, said, "Nazism had fire. Communism has fire, and the Church must catch fire!"

We need some fire in our churches today. I don't mean shouting. I don't even mean yelling "amen." I mean that expectancy, that enthusiasm, that urgency, that fervor which the early Church had.

They had seen a risen Savior. They went out to tell the world about it.

Every night we see people coming here, shedding a few tears. Thank God for tears. We have too few tears over sin today, although we have tears about everything else. The Bible says, "Godly sorrow worketh repentance."

There is a change of purpose involved in repentance. It means that you are willing to turn from sin. You may not have power to turn from your sins. Some may have battles with habits of sin even after conversion. I have seen it time after time. But there must be a willingness in the weakest heart to turn from sin.

You must be willing. God does not say you have to turn; He says you must be willing and, if you are willing, He will help you to turn.

Then there must be a change of conduct. Old things must pass away and behold, all things must become new.

Jesus said, "By their fruits ye shall know them." If I see a man who is going on living habitually in sin, I know that man has never been converted.

He does not have a new nature. He may look like a Christian at times. You can take a pig, give him a bath, put a ribbon on him, dress him up, put a little Chanel No. 5 on him, polish his hoofs a little bit, take him in the living room, and put him in a chair. He looks like a wonderful, clean pig.

You say, "Why, this pig is changed. This is a different pig." You open the door and then see what happens. The nature of the pig has never been changed and the pig runs right to the mud puddle. That is where he belongs.

Now take some of you people on Sunday morning. You dress up and put a little halo on your head, and you go to church and sit down and look like a saint.

Everybody says, "Isn't he a fine upstanding citizen!" While you are watching the preacher, you are thinking about "Gunsmoke" the night before.

You reach in your pocket and you pull out a fifty-cent piece. You flip it into the basket, as though you were giving God a tip.

You say, "Lord, here You are; here is Your tip for the week." You get out of church, shake hands with the minister, go home, take the halo off, take your wings off, pick up your pitchfork, and the horns begin to grow again. No change has taken place.

But any change that God makes in your life is a permanent change! Old things pass away; your life is different.

A change takes place when you come to Christ, and God brings about this tremendous transformation that we call the new birth.

Secondly, not only is repentance needed, but faith — and this word *faith* means more than just belief.

I hear a lot of people who go around and say, "Believe in the Lord Jesus Christ and thou shall be saved."

That's true, but you don't know what the word *believe* means. The word *believe* just doesn't get over to us in English. The word *believe* means more than just intellectual faith, because the Bible says, "The devil believes."

Why, the devil is a fundamentalist, and he is orthodox. He believes in Christ. He believes in the Bible. He believes the whole business of religion. He is even in the religion business.

Intellectually, he believes in the dogma, he believes in the creed. But the devil has never been saved and he is not going to heaven. On Sunday morning many of you can recite the Apostles' Creed through without making a mistake.

But I tell you, that is not enough. There must be a real commitment to Christ. There must be a complete surrender to Christ.

Have you done that? Have you come with everything you have and allowed Him to change your life in full surrender?

Can you say, "Jesus is my Savior? I am trusting in Him and Him alone for salvation? I am not trusting in anything or anybody but Christ? By faith I surrender to Him? I am willing to obey Him and follow Him from this moment on?"

Now, you have head belief and heart belief, but your will must also be involved.

You must be willing to say, "I will receive Christ." Christ appeals to the will of men. Jesus said, "Ye will not come to Me that ye might have life." Jesus didn't say you couldn't come. He said, "Ye *will* not come."

You will not come. There are hundreds of you that ought to come and give your life to Christ. But Jesus says, "Ye will not come." You are not willing for your will to be surrendered to the will of Christ.

Jesus said, "If ye are not willing to confess Me before men, I will not confess you before My Father which is in heaven." You will not. You put up a barrier.

Your will does not bend to Him. "If any man will come after me, . . ." said Jesus. Now, the moment that you come to Christ by repentance and by faith, God in a miraculous and glorious way changes your life.

He forgives all the past. He gives you a new nature. He gives you new values and new motives and a new direction for your life. He puts a smile on your face and a spring in your step and a joy in your soul.

Now, He does not remove your problems. In fact, I think after you come to Christ, you may face more problems. But in the midst of your problems there will be peace and grace and strength and a new dimension for living.

Have you been converted? Are you sure of it? If you are not certain, I ask you to come. In the late eighteenth century, William Wilberforce was converted and almost single-handedly broke the shackles of slavery in England.

On November 29, 1785, he was converted, and he wrote in his diary these words: "I am wretched, miserable, blind and naked. What infinite love that Christ should die to save such a sinner as me."

And that night Wilberforce, only twenty-three years of age, gave his life to Christ and changed the whole course of history.

How many of you know the origin of the Y.M.C.A.? Who founded it? In the latter part of the nineteenth century George Williams was converted in England's west country.

He later wrote how he knelt down at the back of an empty shop. "I cannot describe to you the joy and peace which flowed into my soul when first I saw that the Lord Jesus had died for my sins and that they were all forgiven."

I tell you, when you come to Christ — I do not care when it is, I do not care where it is, or how it is — when you come, you will have to come by repentance and faith, trusting in Him and His death and resurrection alone for salvation.

If you haven't come, if you haven't met Christ, I am asking you to do it now.

You may be a member of the church. But you are not sure and you want to settle it. Do it now! . . .

THE SHOCK OF SAINTLINESS

Whenever a public figure speaks urgently and eloquently about personal morality today, people become instantly cynical and disbelieving. Our late twentieth century has been so saturated by exposees and confidential disclosures about people in public office, sexual and ethical indiscretions by theologians, evangelists, movie stars, and vice-presidents, that there is little room for confidence or assurance when we hear the call for morality, a return to decency, a trust in high personal ideals. The living theater of Vietnam, Watergate, and the fresh disclosures of presidential ethics has jaded the public into an almost professional cynicism.

Several years ago I visited with a producer of a network television show, looking to the possibility of being a guest author, interviewed about the new book, *Schweitzer*, which I co-authored with George Marshall. After discussing the highlights of the life of this amazing Christian doctor, musician, philosopher, and preacher in Africa, the producer closed the book and said, "Sorry, not possible to have you on." Why not? "He's just too good to be true."

For not a few people covering public events and celebrity personalities, Billy Graham has just been "too good to be true." Yet goodness has never been his claim or plea or argument. He wants to be judged as a person who believes in Jesus Christ, who trusts in God and the message of the Word, and has the audacity to bring this gospel to a cynical and unbelieving world.

Several of the most revealing examples of Billy's earnestness and persuasive talents came during the first London Crusade in 1954. Much of the British press was braced for Billy's arrival with the determination of townspeople ready to repel a Norman invasion. Many of the powerful secular press considered Graham about as welcome as a killer shark in the English Channel. Alistair Cooke dumped pages of putdown phrases on the Crusade effort. The big guns of the *Manchester Guardian* under the coaching of the publisher treated Billy like an outbreak of the Asian flu. *Christian Century* let their London correspondent understand that a hatchet job was the order of the day. (Cecil Northcott had been caught squarely in the middle of the critical stance of the *Century*, impressed as he was by personal observation of the Graham Crusades. Crusades had a momentous impact on Britain; Northcott became fascinated by the personality and winsomeness of the American preacher.)

After these columnists had ripped away at his style and the content of his message, Graham surprised the leading British publishers by not only accepting their dinner invitation, but also spending a full evening of terribly frank discussions, answering their most probing — and at times insulting — queries. The directness and candor of the Crusade leader was "damn convincing." Afterward Northcott asked Bevan of the *Manchester Guardian* if he should report on the favorable personal side of Graham, revealing the friendliness, cordiality, and candor. "No," said Bevan, "just cover the public aspect of the evangelist."

It is our claim that such an approach will no longer wash, that reporters must project integrity of a whole person. There are no surprises in Billy's life — no scandals from a staffer, no intrigue or dirty tricks about to be exposed. Graham's continuing success of twenty-five years in public life is based on the strength and surety of twenty-five years of private life that matches the public image. To say this is to touch the heart of the Christian life, its wholeness and its joy. For dozens of years this has been the unceasing observation of people in touch with the personality of Billy

Graham. Television hosts, newspaper editors, university scholars, and airline personnel have come away with a sense of surprise and satisfaction: to meet and know such a global celebrity who carries so gently the fame and so carefully the mission is worth reporting. R. E. C. Browne put this in a way which aptly describes what we are trying to say. He wrote that the "preacher is ultimately known for something other than skill with words. It is holding fast to sound doctrine that makes his skill with words possible and the patterns he weaves into them meaningful; *what he does when he is not making sermons gives his sermons life.*"

The staying power of Billy's influence comes from the center of his life. It was apparent to Dr. David H. C. Read, who was Chaplain to Edinburgh University when Billy made his first British appearance. Writing in *Atlantic Monthly,* Read admitted, "I had not the slightest idea what to expect. His first remarks revealed an attractive voice, a pleasant personality, and a sense of humor." Then Billy announced his theme, "Justification by Faith," and

> launched into a forty-five-minute rapid-delivery exposition. . . . I sat entranced — not because of any unusual brilliance of thought or language; on the contrary I had just written a book, *The Communication of the Gospel,* in which I had suggested that the time had come for a radically new vocabulary and method of preaching for this age; but here was a man using all the battered phrases of evangelism, basing his address on a theological dogma supposed to be meaningless to the average man and communicating as no one I had ever heard.[1]

When Dr. Read returned to his study after this experience at a Graham preaching event for a British audience, he asked himself the question,

> How was it done? There was a directness and a sympathy that struck through the conventional phrases; there was an undoubted charm; the voice was pleasant. But one thing stood out: the man was genuine. He believed what he said. He was concerned about God and the people in front of him and not chiefly with Billy Graham.[2]

This concern for God and people has been unceasing in the life of the evangelist. His celebrity status is secure, for he is known to millions upon millions. However, his desire is that the message and person of Jesus Christ be known and accepted, not the grandfather from Montreat.

The world which sees Graham entirely under the blazing lights of a studio or in front of a stadium throng or a Times Square crowd would be more surprised to know that he often preaches to a dozen or two families in the back-country, dirt-road counties of North Carolina on a Sunday morning. If one is called to preach, "he should rejoice in that call and that privilege." So Billy is the supply preacher for quiet congregations in the back hills of North Carolina.

Twenty years ago Graham was invited to look in at No. 10 Downing Street and its gloomy occupant, the prime minister, Sir Winston Churchill. These were bleak days for the British Commonwealth, and Graham found the national leader depressed and discouraged. They had barely begun talking when the politician of *Blood, Sweat and Tears* asked Billy, "Young man, do you have any hope for the world?" The evangelist reached for his pocket New Testament and quickly responded, "Would you like for me to read some passages? Mr. Prime Minister, this book is full of hope." For a half-hour Graham read to the British leader appropriate passages suited for the time. When he finished, Churchill said, "I thank you. You have given an old man a renewal of faith for the future." In characteristic style, Graham wrote in *Reader's Digest* "I hadn't, the Bible had."

People who have known Graham over a period of years believe that his consistency and timeliness are hallmarks of his ministry. Yet we shall see that he has indeed changed, has adapted to circumstances, and continues to have a contemporary touch that is most unique for a man nearing sixty.

Michael Garde, a convert to Christianity when Billy preached at Earls Court, London, in 1966, covered the Crusade in Minneapolis in 1973. His report was precise: "His illustrations, whether biblical, historical, or topical, explode in the mind with a freshness of new morning." For those who know Graham best, the explosion is nothing less than the Spirit of God moving through one of His saints.

CHAPTER 9

The Gift of Tomorrow

CHAPTER 9

The Gift of Tomorrow

During the Democratic convention of 1976, Rosalynn Carter was asked by a reporter why people should support her husband for President. She smiled and immediately noted that her "man" was an outstanding person, could be counted on to look after the needs and interests of the American republic, was honest and a person of integrity. And then without smiling, she concluded, "You know, there are no scandals in Jimmy's life. I mean, everybody in Plains, Georgia, all six hundred of them — they all know Jimmy and there are no secret scandals, no shame to hide. You won't be surprised in the morning about the conduct of his life."

There are no surprises in Billy Graham's life. There is a private life and there are heartbreaks and setbacks and disappointments and sorrows. Just like your life. His physical stamina — disguised by the towering height, the flashing smile, the year-round tan — cannot be described as powerful. Graham has suffered a large number of ailments: a continuing disability from kidney stones, a recurrent back ailment, and the almost ever-present intestinal flu. Violent attacks of the latter curtailed planned Crusades in Greece and the Philippines in recent years.

Perhaps the biggest surprise to outsiders is the strength and force of Ruth Bell Graham. Billy gets all the coverage or most of it, and that is okay with Ruth. As a college student at Wheaton, she was impressed, if not overwhelmed, by this serious talker from "down South." Listening to him pray with a team of young people about to embark on Sunday mission work, she said to herself, "That's a man who knows God in a very unusual way."

It seems to have been love at first sight for both, for after their first date, Ruth remembered that "for all his terrific dedication and drive, there was a winsomeness about him and a consideration for other people, which I found very endearing."

And Billy found one who could not only fulfill his hopes as a marriage partner, but also bring stability and direction to a large family that needed these qualities while he was absent in their children's formative years. Ruth was kind and firm. Early in their courtship Billy urged Ruth to unite with the Baptist Church, especially since she had not been immersed but had only a Presbyterian sprinkling. Ruth quietly studied the Scriptures, prayed about the matter, and discussed it with her father. Her conclusion was absolute and direct — she would remain a Presbyterian. And she would marry Billy Graham. Her dual loyalty brought a special dimension to the young evangelist — as did the counsel and advice of his missionary-doctor father-in-law.

Some time ago La Piana, the able church historian at Harvard, gave this summary of the three stages that the world's great religions appear to pass through: the ethical is first, followed by the theological, succeeded in turn by the aesthetic. Dr. Theodore Ferris observed,

> They begin with a tremendous moral impulse; then they go through the reflective period when they think through the meaning of their experience, and finally they come to the aesthetic stage when their buildings, their music, and their worship elaborate and flourish as our religion has in hundreds of magnificent buildings. . . . We wonder whether we have reached the third stage.[1]

If anything is happening at all in the Graham preaching of this century, it is a clear call to return to the first stage of a glorious and marching faith. Graham is not beyond the attractiveness of the soaring cathedral, the artistic windows, and dazzling appointments, and into the arena of the world with its open stadium and secular trappings to bring the urgency of Christ's call for discipleship and devotion.

Many of Graham's critics have been uncomfortable with his altar call — the appeal to make a decision for Christ "before it is too late," his insistence that a personal, immediate response is required before God's judgment descends. Some Christians become not only uncomfortable but angry when presented with such a proposition.

While studying this aspect (and it is the most prominent in the Graham presentation of the gospel), I came across these lines:

> "For he is like a refiner's fire"
> He is not coming to soothe you or to comfort you, or to protect you or to insure you against every calamity that may happen to you. He is coming to refine your life; he is coming to burn out the baser metals so that the silver that is there can shine. This is a painful process.[2]

You know what it is like in many different areas of life. You know that a surgeon often has to remove a diseased organ before the body can be well. You don't like to go through that, but sometimes you must. You know that a person often has to root out a poisonous fear or a jealousy or lust or selfishness before he can be a healthy, mature person. And you know that a nation has to be purged of internal hatred and bitterness before it can be strong. This has to happen, and if a person doesn't do it for himself or a nation doesn't do it for itself, something will happen that will get rid of the baser metals so that the pure one can shine in all its splendor.

This is austere and we don't like to hear it. Most of us like to say, "That's the Old Testament; in the New Testament God is love and not judgment. In the New Testament there isn't any austerity like that; in the New Testament the refiner's fire has been burnt out" (the refiner's fire described in Malachi).

But can you say that there is no judgment in love? Is there any love, even in the purely human framework, that is totally without judgment? Is there any love of a parent for a child that is totally lacking in what we call judgment, that desire to refine the life of the child the parent loves?

In the love of a husband or wife, is there no judgment of the other person? *Love without judgment is indulgence, and judgment without love is cruelty.*

I include the following portion of a sermon delivered by one of the leading Episcopal clergymen of the mid-twentieth century, Dr. Theodore Ferris of Trinity Church, Boston. Here is a prominent preacher, a pastor in the theologically liberal heartland (practically across the street from Harvard), who presents a biblical theme of God's judgment with the same cutting zeal that has been attributed to the Southern evangelist. When men and women are honest to the judgment of the New Testament, Ferris proclaims,

> you cannot get away from it. There comes a time when the Lord comes to every human being, whatever you call him or whatever you think about him. If you are young and dislike this language, use some other language. When the Lord comes, he comes sometimes like a father, to heal and to help, to protect, to encourage, to give you strength to carry on. Is there anyone who hasn't known something like that at some time in his life?
>
> There are other times when he comes like a refiner's fire, because there are things in you that have to be burned out before you can be the person you are meant to be. This is painful. There is always fire in the Father's love, and the Father's love is always in the fire.[3]

If there is any single factor in Graham's staying power and the steady extension of his global ministry, it is in his determination to keep sharp the cutting edge of the gospel. For Billy, the blade is the New Testament demand that men and women make a decision about their spiritual life before all is lost. Karl Barth once told Billy to press on with his insistence for a personal response from the audience. Barth had heard the evangelist in Germany, and after the meeting defended Billy's use of emotion to enhance his altar call. Aware that such a response could be fleeting and temporary, the theological giant said,

> Mr. Graham, don't ever let anybody criticize you for the fact that it doesn't last, because for one fleeting moment in that person's life

he stood before God. That will always remain with him to his dying day; he will never forget that one moment when he stood before God."[4]

THE TEAM SPIRIT

As Billy Graham looks back on a quarter-century of world ministry through evangelism, we should identify his success as being carefully supported by an outstanding Team. And the amazing fact about this Team is that these men and women were able to grow with Graham and grow together as a cohesive working agency. Religious organizations are vulnerable to all the temptations, foibles, and mishaps that afflict any other business group. The extra dimension of religious motivation does not preclude the temptations to power, the corporate jealousies and backbiting, and the need for promotion and recognition.

Central to Billy's successful ministry are the years of loyal service of people like George Beverly Shea, the first staff member to be hired by Graham back in the Chicago radio days. Cliff Barrows — song leader, choir director, and emcee of Crusade events — was with Billy during the Youth for Christ era — also joined by the Wilson brothers, T. W. and Grady. T. W. has been an associate evangelist for the past thirty years. Grady is traveling companion, bodyguard, and sought-after speaker for men's breakfasts and cowboy meetings out West.

The business genius from those early formative years is George Wilson, administrative executive for the Minneapolis headquarters and overseer of the booming $30 million annual budget that supports radio and television programs, *Decision* magazine, and the vast fund-raising effort that touches some six million donors in the United States and overseas.

There is no doubt that the early visions of mass evangelism haunted the young evangelistic Team and came to a head during the early failure in California. The effort was known simply as Graham-Barrows in 1948. The two men entered a long night of soul-searching, followed by a critical evaluation of all known techniques of evangelism. Their growth began at the beginning, with this capacity not only to look at their own failures but also to probe the indulgences and flaws of prior personalities in this field of Christian outreach.

Their self-appraisal was shared in depth with Grady Wilson and Bev Shea, and the first thing they all agreed on was that the love-offering had to go. They also identified other aspects of their ministry that required correction; "Sensationalism, over-emotionalism, the tendency to digress on prophecy and to enter controversy, anti-intellectualism as well as the failure to follow up on converts, and the image of being considered anti-church and competitive with local pastors." When Graham understood these perils and proceeded to correct them, his ministry was on the high road of fantastic accomplishment.

HELPING THE CHURCH TO ADVANCE

Graham's achievement in local Crusades is not great mystery. His Team does not accept an invitation to a city or metropolitan area without broad Christian support. Most Crusades are planned eighteen months, even two years in advance. Local sponsors work with the Team on the size of the budget and the early preparations of prayer groups as well as business and professional undergirding. Local pastors are invited at the start to study the goals of the campaign, and the financial pro-jections are approved. When Billy finally arrives at a community, the clergy are the first group assembled after the usual airport press conference.

Billy seems most relaxed and comfortable with fellow clergy. His humor is off and running. His interest in *their* work, *their* problems, *their* aspirations for the coming Crusade is paramount.

On a typical occasion, Billy tells a group of three hundred pastors in New Mexico that he was on a plane trip when a heavy-drinking passenger got out of hand. In desperation a seat-mate tried to quiet the noisy drunk by saying, "Listen, you've got to settle down and be quiet — why that's Billy Graham sitting right there in a seat ahead of you." With that admonition, the wavering passenger turned to Billy Graham and asked, "Are you the evangelist?" "Yes, I am." "Well, put her there, pal, your sermons have sure helped me!" Laughter. Another story, more laughter. And then Billy describes for his on-board audience what the results will be — what their expectations should be for the coming week of meetings in the arena.

"Nine things will happen in this community," the evangelist proposes. "People are praying all over this city for the success of this series of meetings. [More than 1,200 women were already participating in neighborhood prayer groups.] Christians will demonstrate a unity not seen in this city before." The evangelist continues, his voice rising to the far corners of the room. "The Word of God will be preached. People will be converted. Christians will be rededicated. Young people will attend in great numbers. People will debate religion all over the city. Opposition to our Crusades will be heard. The problems of youth will be discussed and satisfied."

The result is that Graham's ministry fulfills the projections made at the beginning. All bills are paid, and a small surplus goes to assist in overseas relief and additional support for the telecast of the Crusade event on network programming during prime time.

Perhaps most important is the fact that the Graham Crusade has brought Christian leaders together in a successful event, unmarked by sharp divisions or unrelenting controversies. Congregations demonstrate a new vitality, higher church attendance, and a more forceful presence in community awareness. When Graham leaves, he leaves behind people with a pleasant and refreshing spiritual awakening — but more than that, he leaves knowing he can return at any time and gain an immediate, enthusiastic audience. A printed one-page flyer gives the gist of the budget for local donors:

THE NEW MEXICO
BILLY GRAHAM CRUSADE

Out of great concern and interest a committee of religious, civic and business leaders have invited Evangelist Billy Graham and his Team to conduct a major crusade to be held in the University Lobo Arena, March 16-23. The spiritual impact of this crusade could provide a moral bulwark against the tidal wave of crime and confusion so prevalent in our society. This spiritual awakening could bring forth enlightened leaders to guide our people back to God. Everyone knows that a Crusade of this magnitude does not just happen.

It takes weeks of prayerful and careful planning and it does cost money. Hundreds are working and praying. Hundreds are needed to contribute financially. The religious and community leaders supporting this endeavor kindly ask for your considerate and generous financial support.

University Lobo Arena
March 16-23

CRUSADE FINANCES

- The extensive preparation necessary to carry on a crusade of this significance requires a lot of money. The proposed budget as shown provides not only for the actual crusade meetings but for five months of extensive preparation and a sufficient period of follow-up.

- Dr. Billy Graham receives no remuneration from this crusade. He is paid an annual salary by the Billy Graham Evangelistic Association with headquarters in Minneapolis, Minnesota. Salaries and expenses for other members of the Team are pro-rated to the time spent in the crusade area. Apart from this and some printed materials, the entire budget will be disbursed in this area.

- The Billy Graham Crusade, Inc. has been organized under New Mexico law expressly for this crusade. It is entirely responsible for the subscription and expenditure of all crusade funds and is organizationally separate and completely apart from the Billy Graham Evangelistic Association Incorporated.

- All donations are income tax deductible. A complete post-crusade audit will be made by a local accounting firm, and the audit statement will be published in the local press with additional copies available upon request.

- Personal checks may be made payable to: New Mexico Billy Graham Crusade, Inc.

OPERATING BUDGET

ADMINISTRATION Office Rent, Supplies, Furniture, Equipment and Personnel	$ 49,100
ARRANGEMENTS Auditorium, Rent, Utilities, Public Address System, Light and Stage Personnel	43,000
ADVERTISING/PUBLICITY Newspapers, Radio, Television, Billboards	24,500
INVITED TEAM PERSONNEL Travel, Housing, Salaries	32,050
SPECIAL ITEMS Materials, Films, Meetings, Luncheons	13,000
COMMITTEE EXPENSES/PROJECTS Materials, Printing, Processing, Mailing, Meetings	43,350
TOTAL	$205,000

THE GIFT OF TOMORROW

America was born out of religious revivals. The impulse which brought the first settlers to our land was founded on a deeply felt spiritual commitment, prominently expressed by the pilgrims and institutionalized by the Puritans. The Calvinistic theology of the first century of settlement finally exploded in the determined preaching of Jonathan Edwards around 1740 and was reinforced by the arrival of George Whitefield. The "Great Awakening" was the term applied to this American revival, which went on for decades and finally gave emotional force to the Revolutionary War. A significant missionary thrust was generated by these tent meetings, first to the new Western settlements and then to overseas and distant continents.

A century later, in the 1830s, the "Great Revivals" erupted under the inspired preaching of Charles Finney. A staggering amount of moral energy flowed from these national and regional meetings, later described by Gilbert Barnes in his study of Theodore Weld, considered by many to be the real mastermind of the abolitionists' lobby in the North. Barnes wrote,

> The agitation was accomplished not so much by heroes of reform as by very numerous obscure persons, prompted by an impulse, religious in character and evangelical in spirit, which began in the Great Revival of 1830 — and translated into anti-slavery organizations.[5]

Weld was converted to Christianity by the preaching of Finney at Utica, New York. He went on to marry antislavery activist (and Southerner) Angelina Grimke. Finney was to found Oberlin College and become a strong advocate for minority education and women's rights. But all this social and humanitarian expression traces its beginnings to the Great Revivals of Charles Finney.

Now we come to the mid-twentieth century and the "Great Crusades" of Billy Graham. Much has been written about the Moody-Sankey revivals of the late nineteenth century and the singular effort of Billy Sunday and Homer Rodeheaver shortly thereafter. But none of these can approach the size and scope of the Graham Crusades, which may prove to be the most enduring in American history.

In addition to millions touched with the gospel and thousands reported to have made decisions for Christ, what can we expect as a lasting result of the Graham ministry to this part of the twentieth century, in this part of the world?

1. Billy Graham has become, through his Crusades, a living bridge for conservative and liberal Christians. His movement and meetings have provided a place for encounter not combat; created an atmosphere of belonging instead of battle. This was desperately needed within the wider Protestant community, for each of the major Christian divisions harbored much suspicion and animosity toward one another.

The late E. Stanley Jones, the Methodist missionary to India who was so greatly beloved in almost every segment of the wider Christian community, caught early the significance of the Graham evangelistic successes. His writings in the 1950s helped to interpret to both liberals and conservatives the dynamic role that Graham already was fulfilling for the people of God.

Dr. Jones pointed to the controversies that swirled around Graham and argued that the Church was witnessing Hegel's thought in action — thesis, antithesis, and synthesis. According to Jones, the truth of American Christianity was moving toward a new reality, forged in the debates over Graham's persuasive influence, by both wings of Protestantism.

"Both groups want to share Christ," wrote the missionary of India (and close friend of Gandhi),

> in differing terminology and in differing methods, but neverthe-
> less, both want to share Christ. The synthesis is emerging at a very
> important place — at evangelism. There the conservative and
> liberal could join in the only place they could get together — at the
> place of making Christ known to people inside and outside the
> churches who need conversion. That synthesis is a good one, the
> best possible one.
>
> This coming together, as in all such cases, will be opposed by
> two groups: the radical conservatives and the radical liberals. . . .

Both of them will see in it compromise, not comprehension, . . . both attacking Graham in newspapers. However, the rest of the main body of conservatives and liberals, tired of acrid fundamentalism and acrid liberalism, see in this Crusade a symptom of the possibility of working together to win men for Christ and have eagerly and rightly embraced it.[6]

Jones concluded that out of this coalition something very exciting might emerge — the Christian.

Movements have flourished, fads have blossomed and faded — and Graham has enlarged and extended his ministry as the bridge where Christians could gather and talk and reach out to the lost and broken and negligent.

2. The Graham Crusades held a steady course while mainline churches went through almost self-destructive convulsions. As a result, millions of church members were steadied and supported by his public ministry, fulfilling needs and yearnings of believers when local pastors were cracking up or breaking down or sinking into confusions of the turbulent sixties and cynical seventies.

I have met countless people who regularly watch the Graham rallies on television. They never send letters of appreciation or gifts of financial support, but we must number in the thousands those who admit that Billy speaks to their condition and moves them by his spiritual insight. They are church members in good standing, even active in local leadership, but quietly and personally they have found their sustaining religious experience in the Graham meetings viewed in some distant city or country. Graham is the universal spokesman for Christianity.

3. Few of us have been untouched by the celebrations and enthusiasm generated by bicentennial observances in the United States. Something more than patriotism and something more lasting than "civil religion" was happening to millions of citizens. For many it was a recovery of the dynamic vitality that shaped this country at the beginning. If this is a nation under God, there are tens of thousands who are prepared to respond to a moral and ethical reawakening that was such a force for the founding fathers.

Graham's preaching for years has been calling believers to the fulfillment of a righteous nation, a new Jerusalem of hope, a new Zion of accountability before God. After the civil assassinations of the fifties and sixties, the hell of Vietnam, and the shame of Watergate, great numbers of people with or without a Christian heritage are open and receptive to the urgency of Graham's Great Crusade. His message is relevant in a real world of depravity, lust, hatred, and disillusionment. Billy spoke to this convincingly in his message, "Four Great Crises," in preparation for 1976:

Throughout 200 years of American history our country has weathered many crises, but four of them stand out above the rest. The first one took place during the Revolutionary War. We didn't even know whether or not we could be born. It was my privilege to be present when President Eishenhower made a speech at Valley Forge, in which he said, "This is where they got it for us." The winter of 1777-1778 was a terrible time for the ragtag American soldiers. Food, clothing, even water, were in short supply. Pestilence moved in. Thousands of soldiers died of starvation, exposure, disease. When General Washington received word that a British force had left Philadelphia and was marching in his direction, he ordered his troops mobilized and was told that they could not stir from their huts. They were too weak to move.

In the midst of that winter George Washington was reported seen on his knees in the snow, calling upon God for help. Out of that winter of tribulation Washington led his exhausted, discouraged, tattered army to victory. It took three more years to achieve, but it brought the independence of the United States. I believe God helped that little army all the way to Yorktown.

The next great crisis in American history came a few years later when a convention was summoned to Philadelphia to draft a constitution for the new country that was being born. The weather was warm, tempers were flaring, and the convention was getting nowhere. Some were for picking up their hats and leaving for home. The future of America was in the balance.

At that moment, on June 2, 1787, a delegate from Pennsylvania, Benjamin Franklin, rose to his feet. "Mr. President," he said, "we indeed seem to feel our own want of political wisdom, since we have been running all about in search of it. How has it happened, sir, that we have not hitherto once thought of humbly applying to the Father of Lights to illuminate our understandings? We have been assured, sir, in the Sacred Writings that "except the Lord build the house, they labor in vain that build it." I firmly believe this. I therefore beg leave to move that henceforth prayers, im-

ploring the assistance of heaven and its blessing on our delibera-
tions, be held in this assembly every morning before we proceed
to business."[7]

No action was taken on Franklin's request, but within three
weeks the deadlock was broken and the Constitution was adopted.
Men did pray, and their prayers helped, I believe, to give us that
immortal document, the Constitution of the United States.
Perhaps as an indirect result of Franklin's speech, both houses of
Congress are traditionally opened with prayer each day while in
session.

The third great crisis came during the Civil War. While men on
both sides were killing each other, brother sometimes standing
against brother, it seemed our little country would be torn apart.
We threatened to become two separate nations. So weakened had
we become that it even looked as if some European power might
take us over. But there were men and women on both sides who
believed in God.

General Daniel E. Sickles reports that President Abraham Lincoln told him that during the Gettysburg campaign, "I went to my
room one day and locked the door and got down on my knees
before almighty God. . . . And after that a comfort crept into my
soul that God had taken the whole business into his own hands and
that things would go right."[8] After Gettysburg, and on two other
occasions during the Civil War, Lincoln called the entire American nation to a special day of prayer, fasting, humiliation, and
thanksgiving.

THE FOURTH CRISIS

As for General Robert E. Lee, someone asked him one day,
"Aren't you praying for victory?" and the general replied, "No, I'm
praying that the will of God be done." We believe that God's will
was done. The shackles of slavery were thrown off, the union was
preserved, and the nation reunited.

The fourth great crisis in American history was not World War I.
Our security was never threatened in that war, nor was it
threatened in World War II. Despite the tragic loss of life, we
were never really threatened as a nation during that war either.
The fourth great crisis in American history is the crisis of the
present moment. Our nation is being threatened today as it has
not been threatened since the Civil War. It is not that we are being
menaced by Communism, although that danger is with us from
within and without. Something even more serious is taking place
in America. It is moral deterioration.

Ever since the end of World War II this country, along with the other English-speaking countries, has been plunging into moral corruption at a rate that is gaining momentum. Honesty and truthfulness have been thrown out the window. The United States of America is on one mad whirl of amusements and pleasure and licentiousness and immorality. Juvenile delinquency is mounting so rapidly we can't keep pace with the figures. The drug menace, far from decreasing, is increasing, and claiming new young victims every day. The latest FBI crime figures are shocking: a 12 per cent increase in violent crimes. Chronic alcoholics number at least six million.

Some of the identical symptoms that were noticed in Rome during the last days of the Empire are now observed and felt in our society. Divorce rates are increasing. Racial tensions are worse, not better. Inflation is siphoning off the savings of those with lower incomes. Political issues are dividing us. Confidence in government has been shaken. Walk down the streets of our cities and read the names of the latest films on the marquees. Most of the films deal with sex, crime, and abnormal behavior. One can only ask, what is the country coming to?

FALSE RELIGION

I tell you, we need a moral revival. We need a spiritual revival that will put a new moral fiber into our society. As things are, we are being softened up for the kill. We will be done for before the Communist troops ever get here. It is time that we come to the foot of the cross. When we come to the cross and receive Christ as Savior, he gives us the capacity to love our neighbor. There is no superior race in God's sight. God does not look upon the outward appearance, he looks upon the heart. God sees our pride. We will have to come where we can love each other as neighbors and look through the eyes of Jesus at these problems.

One of the biggest dangers to the Western world today, as I see it, is false religion. The cults are flourishing. Now, God says you can have all the religion you want. I'm not going to hear your prayers because you don't mean what you say. It doesn't come from the heart. Thousands of people in our churches are serving God with their lips, but their hearts are far from him. They have never had an encounter with Jesus Christ, have never been born again, have never been converted.

God is looking for real and genuine repentance. "To whom much is given, of him will much be required."[9] Much has been given to America and much shall be required of her. God cannot send a revival until we pay the price. America can be spared, but only in God, only be renewed through individual repentance and faith in him.

THE GREAT NEED

Why has God spared us this long? There are several reasons. First, it is found in the very nature of God. The Bible teaches that God is a God of mercy, long-suffering, and full of love. Every time I look at the cross, where he gave his Son to shed his blood for our sins, I see written over it in letters of fire, "God is love, God is love, God is love, he loves you, he loves you, he loves you." He is not willing that any should perish. God does not want you to go to hell. But if you will not come to Christ, there is nothing God can do. You can say "no" or "yes" to God, either one; it's all up to you.

I believe too that God is prospering our nation because of the great number of born-again Christians in our midst. If it were not for God's people, America would have been in hell long ago. It's the Lord's people whom God is honoring. Don't despise that godly Christian who lives next door to you. Don't laugh at that Christian student who goes to school with you. He is one of the reasons this nation has the blessings and prosperity that it has. But unless the Lord's people can discipline themselves to prayer and Bible study and the living of a Spirit-filled, Christ-honoring life, that blessing will not last very long.

I am convinced that our nations are in peril. The handwriting is on the wall. The signs of the times are everywhere. We cannot continue long in our moral degeneracy. A cancer is eating at the heart and core of our society. We need to humble ourselves, for no one can come proudly to the Kingdom of God. If you have never come to Christ, the only prayer you can really pray is, "God, be merciful to me, a sinner."[10] Have you prayed that prayer?

The great need today is not for more guns or more atomic bombs. The need is for men and women who have been transformed by the power of Christ and are living dedicated lives for Christ in the office, the factory, the shop, the home, and taking their stand for the Lord Jesus Christ, no matter what the cost may be. They alone will lead us out of the fourth great crisis in our national life.

BILLY'S GIFT — THE INVITATION

If Billy Graham is surprised by the astonishing developments in his own life and the soaring success of his preaching ministry, he humbly attributes these achievements to staying close to the Bible in the message he proclaims. He admits to a divine call that has not faded, although it frequently has been tested. One time NBC offered him a million dollars a year to perform opposite the

Arthur Godfrey show; Godfrey was big-time in the fifties and dominated the morning-show ratings.

Billy once told Ted Fiske of *The New York Times* that he believed absolutely that God had called him to a special ministry at a special time in history. "If anything bothers me," he added, "it is the thought that at Judgment Day I may find that I have not been as faithful as some other minister who is slugging it out day after day with few visible achievements in a storefront in Harlem." The evangelist believes that all Christians are given gifts by the Holy Spirit, as outlined by the apostle Paul. Does he have a special gift? The answer is direct and affirmative:

> At the invitation I believe that God has given me this gift in asking people to come forward and make a commitment to Christ at the end of my sermons. And in the several minutes that this appeal lasts [he urges people to come forward, reminding them that their friends or the buses or the traffic will wait] . . . while I am standing there, not saying a word, it's when most of my strength leaves me. I have no explanation for that, but I become exhausted and experience something going out of my being.[11]

If there is any meaning at all in the Graham ministry, now and in the future, it is the public witness of one who believes that God acts in history, that His will can be known by men and women, and that salvation is a joyous, contagious revelation. Graham's emphasis on centrality of the person of Jesus Christ and the primacy of the Holy Bible has neither waned nor faltered in the preaching and teaching of the evangelist. The unwavering witness is important; he urged John Corry of *Harper's* to offset the influence of other Christian personalities — not to erase or wipe them out, but to balance them in the eyes of the public:

> Niebuhr is an economic theologian; Tillich is more a philosopher, and Barth, we need more men like him. The trend is toward evangelical theology. Too many ministers think they're social engineers. They even want to get into the business of deciding where the highways go. You must remember that the worst part of history was in the Dark Ages, when the Church ran everything.[12]

And now Niebuhr, Tillich, and Barth are gone. And Graham is correct: evangelical theology is at center stage for the unfolding Christian drama.

The Legacy of Billy's Warning to America

CHAPTER 10

The Legacy of Billy's Warning to America

Returning the gospel to the people — the Church to the laity — is one of the significant by-products of the Graham era. And the unique strategy to fulfill such a movement has been to lift up the local pastor: Graham has initiated hundreds of conferences for thousands of clergymen to assist them in their ministry and pastoral labors. Every other evangelist in modern history has been held under suspicion by local clerics — or at least studied with large reservations. Graham's public presentation and quiet personal endeavor has resulted in the strengthening and assisting of the pastor in his parish. He has accomplished this in several ways.

First of all, Billy has urged a return to the Bible for converts and new Christians. Every significant and growing Christian church today is centered around Bible study. Graham's organization has promoted this effort in every way imaginable — through study programs by mail, for example and through direct sale of new translations. (Probably half of the thirteen million copies of *The Living Bible* have gone to individuals introduced to this contemporary version by Graham's promotion.)

By putting the burden of inquiry and growth on the new Christian, Billy has detached himself, his personality, and his interpretations and has directed the seeker to the Scriptures. It was Chesterton who said that men in a state of decadence "employ professionals to fight for them, professionals to dance for them, and a professional to rule them." Every person has to do his own praying, studying, and serving under Graham's interpretation of the Christian experience. He may be the messenger, the catalyst, the introducer; but the inquirer has to take it from there. And when he does, it invariably leads to personal Bible study, group participation, and involvement in the local church for worship and praise.

Second, Graham has given immeasurable assistance to the clergy in our time. Most of his major Crusades include a School of Evangelism planned and directed entirely for area clergy. When Billy was in Lubbock, Texas, recently, nearly six hundred men and women of the cloth, including military and institutional chaplains, attended a special seminar headed by the evangelist. When West Coast Christians held a Hollywood Bowl celebration of the twenty-fifth anniversary of Graham's public ministry, the evangelist's organization arranged for hundreds of ministers and their wives to attend a three-day conference in the techniques and skills of contemporary evangelism.

When one considers that there are nearly a quarter million ministers in America and the average congregation is about 275 persons, the professional needs all the input and guidance possible. Graham does not pre-empt denominational studies for pastors, but he clearly goes out of his way to promote their profession and increase their effectiveness. Perhaps long ago he learned that their way and his way are one.

Is Billy different? That question surfaces when historians and students of prior revivals compare Graham to the greats of the past. His critics prefer to link him with the sub-Christian antics of other times and drape him in the color scheme of a Marjo or an Elmer Gantry. But any basis for that comparison, eagerly drawn by some in the first years of Billy's preaching, has all but vanished today. It made marvelous copy for the slick magazines and the late-night talk shows which were always unleashing a fresh sneer at religion. But Billy was beyond this, for he had already studied the dilemmas and searched out the destructive forces that had broken other men in other times.

Billy was — and still is — different. The contrast was seen early in the London Crusades and the Scottish meetings that followed. David H. C. Read caught the essence of this young Southern preacher in the way he conducted himself and his religious campaign. Dr. Read wrote in *Atlantic Monthly,*

> Long before he came to Scotland, the British public had been making up its mind about this young evangelist. The cards were stacked against him when he came. One touch of "I've come to save Britain," one word of criticism of cherished institutions, secular or ecclesiastic, one gesture of insincerity and religious racketeering, and he would have gone to that limbo of hollow laughter the British reserve for such intruders. It took only a few weeks for Billy to disabuse the critics and win for himself a place in the affection of the public that has been given to few foreign guests and to no other visiting evangelist in living memory.[1]

A major part of Billy's difference is found in the absence of a Graham cult. While he is admired by millions of people and supported by millions of dollars, there are no Graham sweat shirts, no Graham shrines, no Graham wrist watches, and very few people quoting Billy Graham like some kind of guru. He has not written a special theology or a comprehensive library of doctrine. He is not interested in promoting his lasting image, but is deeply concerned about advancing the Word of God. When 100,000 young people participated in EUROFEST, a week of Christian inspiration in Brussels, Graham was the featured speaker. Yet no one came away with a Graham calendar or a Billy Graham coloring book or an attractive medallion to wear around the neck or wrist. What they did come away with were some fresh insights into the Christian life and a week of Bible study in seven languages. Billy's difference has been the Church's gain, especially a wide acceptance for a whole new style of evangelism.

"The average duration of a period of revivalistic fervor in the past has been about ten years. If history is any guide, Graham's popularity has about two more years to run." So wrote a college professor in *The Nation* in 1957. Three years later the same writer, William G. McLoughlin, Jr., published a book entitled *Billy Graham, Revivalist in a Secular Age*. This was a thorough and thoughtful study of not only the evangelist but also the impact of revivals in other periods of American history. McLoughlin's closing chapter expresses these sentiments:

> On the whole it now looks as if Billy Graham's revivals have lost their luster. So much has been written about him and his work and each crusade is so similar to all the preceding ones that public curiosity has been satiated. Billy Graham's revivals are no longer news — or at least they are only news when they show signs of not being particularly successful. Furthermore, there are no discernible results of his meetings which seem to merit conspicuous attention.[2]

Even while writing this critique of Graham's influence, McLoughlin agreed that the famous preacher had placed himself on very solid ground in centering his message on the truths and authority of the Bible:

> Because Western civilization in general, and Protestant countries in particular, are so thoroughly imbued with the Judeo-Christian tradition imbedded in the Bible, Graham is on firm ground in using it as the source of his message. The clearest notes in his preaching are his emphasis upon the patriarchal authoritarianism and righteous Jehovah of the Old Testament and his assertion of the individualistic aspects of faith, hope, and love in the New.[3]

Graham's great skill has been not only to know the Scriptures but also to use the Bible in fresh, arresting applications to the needs of the hour. And while liberal interpreters may decry his frequently literalistic presentation, the solid-rock base has delivered Billy from the clutches of his critics. While Billy was hardly vulnerable to the intellectual hobbies of some liberal theologians (such as the God-is-dead movement, given an extra six months' life by a cover story in *Time*), neither was he tripped up by any fascination with speaking in tongues and other manifestations of the charismatic movement which has stirred ecclesiastical unrest in many parts of the country. Graham also steered clear of faith-healing inducements and prophecy controversies — while still holding to the primary doctrines of a conservative theology.

Billy's use of Holy Writ is never more effective than in his best-selling book *Angels: God's Secret Agents.* Long ago he was quoted as believing that "the average religious intelligence of an American is that of a twelve-year-old. Therefore, preaching of today must be in utter simplicity almost as if you were talking to children." In *Angels* the evangelist applies this theory for millions of readers and brings into focus the message of the Bible concerning celestial beings. He uses the theme as a counterbalance to the current rage for occultism, astrology, Satan worship, demon possession, and preoccupation with the devil.

FRANK AND ERNEST By Bob Thaves

© 1976 by Newspaper Enterprise Association, Inc. Used by permission.

Graham noted in his *Angels* introduction that

> just a few years ago such ideas would have been scorned by most educated people. Science was king, and science was tuned into believing only what could be seen or measured. The idea of supernatural beings was thought to be nonsense, the ravings of a lunatic fringe. All this has changed. Think, for example, of the morbid fascination modern society has for the occult.[4]

As cited earlier, Graham had completed a manuscript for his publisher on the subject of the devil, with a working title, *The Cloven Hoof.* When the motion pictures *The Exorcist* and *Rosemary's Baby* broke upon the public with such fury and fascination, Graham refused to publish his book. Many believe that his wife, Ruth, was most influential in urging him not to give the devil so much publicity. As the occult and study of Satanism came on with such intensity, Billy searched for a way to mount a meaningful counterattack.

Graham's proposal was simple and convincing: angels have a much more important place in the Bible than the devil and his demons. "The Bible teaches that angels intervene in the affairs of a nation. God often uses them to execute judgment on nations. They guide, comfort, and provide for the people of God in the midst of suffering and persecution."[5]

Not unexpectedly *Angels* has had a staggeringly successful sale — and the usual head-shaking from scholars who long ago passed the twelve-year-old level of understanding. Yet even for the academics, Graham had some reminders from Calvin:

> Angels are the dispensers and administrators of divine beneficence toward us. They regard our safety, undertake our defense, direct our ways, and exercise a constant solicitude that no evil befall us.[6]

And from Luther:

> An angel is a spiritual creature without a body created by God for the service of christendom and the church.[7]

Again, *Angels* is simply a literary technique that Graham used to promote biblical study and the central authority of the New Testament. In this moment in time he has used a popular issue and turned it to the advantage of Christian proclamation. *Angels* is really a swift survey of the whole Bible, culminating in the life, death, and resurrection of Jesus Christ. Riding on a hot, controversial topic like Satanism, Graham employs nearly six hundred biblical references and the saving power of Jesus Christ.

Angels actually became Graham's disguised vehicle to reach millions of people with the gospel. Graham will be remembered in church history not only for his preaching and Great Crusades, but also for his uncanny timing in seizing a current issue and turning it to Christian advantage.

In the early days of his public ministry, the evangelist was eloquent in his warnings against international communism.

Billy urged a major defense posture against the Red menace.

He frequently echoed phrases from his early hero, J. Edgar Hoover. He warned that America must meet the Communist challenge head-on. With the subsiding of the McCarthy era (and panic) and with extensive overseas travel, even to Russia, Billy began to alter his fierce attacks against the followers of Marx, Lenin, and Stalin. Yet, in *Angels* he reminds us that "there must come a time when God will call upon the Hitlers, the Eichmanns, and the Stalins of this world for an accounting."

Graham illustrated frequently the depravity and fallenness of man in the arrogance and false prophecies of the Marxist doctrine. It was timely, current — and, his critics would add, fashionable. But the world shifted, and the Red peril revealed unexpected weakness as the Russian-Chinese partnership unraveled. Graham has come to the position, again central in Scripture, which Arnold Rogow proposes, that "all human experience, including the history of nations, seems to demonstrate that enemies within are more difficult to conquer than enemies without."

In the early seventies the Graham organization was deeply influenced by the growing number of evangelicals (including Billy's brother-in-law, Leighton Ford) who urged an aggressive stance in social action. Leaders such as Richard Mouw, Carl F. H. Henry, and others produced in 1973 a Thanksgiving statement known as the Chicago Declaration.

> We acknowledge that we have failed to condemn the exploitation of racism at home and abroad by our economic system. . . .
>
> Before God and a billion hungry neighbors, we must re-think our values regarding our present standard of living and promote more just acquisition and distribution of the world's resources. . . . We must challenge the misplaced trust of the nation in economic and military might — a proud trust that promotes a national pathology of war and violence which victimizes our neighbors at home and abroad. We must resist the temptation to make the nation and its institutions objects of near-religious loyalty. . . . We acknowledge that we have encouraged men to prideful domination and women to irresponsible passivity. . . .

Conservative Christians were standing apart from — and actually against — the power pretentions of America. In Billy, they found a companion, friend, and responsive listener.

PROBLEMS CAN BECOME PERILS

As a national religious leader and an internationally acclaimed Christian celebrity, Billy Graham will face two major problems in his ministry in the remaining years of active public appearance.

The first danger is his close identification with other people in public life, especially "the man in the White House." Graham has been received by five Presidents, fairly close to three, and very close to one. In the early seventies the participation of President Nixon and his address at one of Graham's Crusades brought forth questioning wrath from secular critics and cautioning advice from close friends. (Nixon once disclosed that Graham encouraged him to seek public office again after his defeat by John F. Kennedy.)

Many news commentators pointed to Graham as the "White House chaplain" during the Nixon administration (even though over a six-year period he appeared only four times to lead Sunday worship services). The linkage between religion and rulers has always been questionable for both parties.

When Billy appeared at the Honor America Day promoted primarily by the embattled White House occupant, Richard Nixon, *Newsweek* was to make the event a cover story. The editors of that journal concluded that Graham was serving a god of the American state and not the God and Father of Jesus Christ. Wrote one observer, "After 30 years of public preaching, Billy Graham had finally found his proper pulpit — and his proper theme."[8]

The "civil religion" theme has made liberals and conservatives alike uncomfortable. Whatever the right reasons for being available in a chaplaincy role to the Congress or at the President's elbow as his "pastor," Graham has become more and more vulnerable to the charge of giving aid and comfort to the status quo — and the party in power.

The most difficult event is the Presidential Prayer Breakfast (or the Governor's or Mayor's or whoever's), in which the fellowship of Christian pastors with incumbent political leaders presents a strong advertisement of religious support for the people in charge. Graham's intimacy with various Presidents has not been an easy assignment, and the Nixon-Watergate revelations became downright dangerous for the evangelist's credibility. (It is hazardous, in any event, for church leaders to be coupled with heads of state. The Church historically has plunged into deep trouble whenever it has embraced kings, presidents, or dictators. Invariably the rulers' intoxication with power leads to corruption, exposing the Church to the very evils it is required by God to judge and correct. Graham should be in the company of White House pickets, not Presidents, say his critical watchers.)

Presidential breakfasts may be a thing of the past. In most recent feedings, speakers such as U. S. Sen. Mark O. Hatfield made the sponsors so uncomfortable with his outline and charge of "civil religion" that few Christians may wish to be cast in such a compromising stance with the politicians. Another important and significant feature is the news that Graham is no longer going to attend or promote prayer breakfasts for those in public office. Obviously the evangelist has been listening to Hatfield and studying the serious aftereffects of close relationships with any President. It is also significant that the evangelist was not present at *either* party convention in 1976 and very well may never again be seen in an inauguration of a future President — Southern Baptist notwithstanding!

Graham has been concerned that his overseas witness and effectiveness for the cause of Christ have been damaged or delayed by his conversations, associations, and social get-togethers with former Secretary of State Henry Kissinger. Many believe that Graham turned down a Middle East Crusade in 1975 for fear of being slandered as a CIA spokesman or a Kissinger courier. While Billy will probably always be the friend of Presidents and will be welcome at political receptions, his public identification may decline to a very low profile. The Nixon daughters' birthday parties are a thing of the past.

A second problem which may become a pleasant peril for Graham is that of turning into an institution in his own lifetime. So far, Billy has resisted efforts to build a cult around his personality. Yet every prominent artistic, cultural, political, and religious hero-celebrity has close associates with a heavy personal investment in the success of their leader-hero. Graham is surrounded by a powerful and successful Team who have served him well for three decades. Some of these men and women earn salaries of more than $20,000 a year. Those responsible for the creative aspects of radio/television/publishing are justified in their compensation and certainly want it to continue. However, when a movement becomes an institution, with buildings and grounds and investments and trusts, it can lose its nerve and daring, generally turn cautious and calculating, and end up just another establishment on the religious landscape. This represents the largest headache for the internal aspect of the Graham organization.

During the past decade the Graham organization has attracted broad and generous support for its evangelistic activities in North America and overseas. Increasingly, Billy has responded to the urgent requests of Christian leaders to help underwrite the launching of programs for evangelistic outreach in the Third World. As the Billy Graham Evangelistic Association's budgets for Crusades, television programming, and publishing were fully subscribed by donor contributions on a year-to-year basis, surplus amounts were set aside for overseas needs and long-range projects in the United States.

Friends of Graham have urged him to create an evangelistic enterprise, perhaps a center, that would extend his ministry far beyond his active days as a preacher of the Good News. Billy's natural hesitancy about ego-grandeur put the brakes on this notion until he could experience a larger vision of what this really might become — a training center for future pastors, preachers, and evangelists plus a Bible institute to give enrichment and support for Christian men and women as they pursue the life of Jesus Christ.

By 1970 these aspirations and resources blended in the creation of the World Evangelism and Christian Education Fund. Established separately from the Billy Graham Evangelistic Association, the Fund was created as a nonprofit trust to advance the needs of overseas opportunities (such as the Congress on Evangelism held in Berlin) and look ahead to the time of building the institute which would assure Graham's place in contemporary evangelism.

In less than a decade, the Fund — called WECE — under the careful management of William Mead, Dewey Presley, and George Bennet (retired treasurer of Harvard University) grew to nearly $23 million. Friends of Billy's work contributed small and large amounts. Estates and bequests flowed in as well as the five- and ten-dollar contributions that have been the cornerstone of Graham's global effort. Then, just as construction was about to begin on the acquired eight-acre site adjacent to Wheaton College in Illinois, a reporter for the *Charlotte Observer* announced that Billy was sitting on a twenty-million-dollar "secret" fund, that it was hidden from public view, and that it funneled resources into activities close to the evangelist's heart.

As noted earlier, Graham has been steadily pursued by investigative reporters who are persuaded that an organization with so much success and so many available resources must have some greed accounts or indulgence activities blooming somewhere. And the irony is that Billy's success is built on the opposite: his donor support comes from those who trust him because they trust his message in the gospel. When this trust fund discussion became a momentary public item, I asked different individuals about their reaction to the "fresh" information concerning Graham's ministry. Said Eldridge Cleaver,

> Well, last year Kathleen and I watched Billy's telecast during New Year's. It was direct and inspiring. We had just opened a new checking account in Northern California and right then and there I wrote out our first check — $100 — to advance this great Christian's ministry. He knows where it ought to go, and my money is one way of voting in favor of his world mission.

Directors of the WECE Fund told this writer that $15,500,000 will be spent in the next two years on the completion of the Wheaton Center for Biblical Studies and Communications. Additional money will go to student scholarships for those attending overseas Congresses on Evangelism and the final thrust will be a lay training center in the mountains of North Carolina. Those close to the Fund's management, such as William Mead of Dallas, have anticipated that another $25 million will be required to complete all of these projects. This writer suspects that these funds will be gathered in the next five years because, as Cleaver put it, it's one way of voting in favor of Graham's world mission.

Some unusually creative people have had large enough visions to project satisfying and enduring institutions. Finney gave much to Oberlin. Moody established Northfield and Mount Hermon, two of the finest Christian prep schools in the world. Chautauqua flourishes institutionally, but many places have faded once the original personality or impulse was gone from the scene. Graham's peril is similar to Albert Schweitzer's — becoming a legend and being served by legendary sages that blunt the vitality or creativeness of the personality who combined nerve and risk for a dynamic ministry. Loving and protective and possessive associates can build the most attractive tombs. . . .

THE BURDEN OF BEING BLESSED

If Graham has the talents and skills and success of an established world ministry, he has also the special burden that comes with such an attainment. Comments and quotes are continually sought — and frequently rejected. He may be considered a spokesman for the whole Christian community and enjoy great visibility and popularity, yet he has never had the capacity or the desire to be the philosopher or brain for the whole Christian enterprise. The smoothness of his organization and the polish of his presentation will always cause some within the intelligentsia to express suspicion in biting terms. Philip Terzian said of Charles Colson's conversion, "I, for one, have an admittedly fastidious antipathy to the whole phenomenon of 'born again,' couched as it is in the simplistic terms and generally presided over by charlatans like Billy Graham."[9]

Billy is prepared to carry the burden, to press on with a ministry that never will be completed — yet always satisfying:

As an evangelist I have often felt too far spent to minister from the pulpit to men and women who have filled stadiums to hear a message from the Lord. Yet again and again my weariness has vanished, and my strength has been renewed. I have been filled with God's power not only in my soul but physically. On many occasions God has become especially real, and has sent His unseen angelic visitors to touch my body to let me be His messenger for heaven, speaking as a dying man to dying men.[10]

The other part of the burden for one who is blessed is the adulation of the public and the incessant praise of friends. Louis Zamperini tells about a get-together at the Graham home, an informal evening with prominent clergy friends from around the country. Louis recalls, "One friend who opened the proceedings built up Billy so high that all eyes were glued on this second Elijah. Then Billy began and turned everygody's eyes off himself without being too obvious about it; and when he got through, everybody was Christ-conscious — so much so that during the discussion nobody noticed when Billy Graham left the room."[11]

Billy endures the burden of what he is in the eyes of the world by pointing people to Christ. This is his gaze and goal, and in a natural way he brings others to the same panorama of faith. Anything less would have been self-corrupting, and the charlatan label would have been correctly applied.

Ruth Graham said of her preacher partner: "Billy is constantly thinking, planning, how best in the short time we have left to present the world with the claims of Christ and the hope that is to be found in the everlasting Gospel. Big Thoughts, big plans. . . . He carries the world in his heart."

VERY PERSONAL

Often the real personality is seen in fleeting scenes, passing episodes that reveal the richness and naturalness of a public figure such as Graham. The sudden smile, the laughter at unexpected goofs, the springing up steps two at a time, the silent stare out a plane window — these signs and gestures proclaim the inner person as loudly as words or sentences.

Companions from the inner circle respect his privacy and

shield their star from the destructive dangers of public possession
and incessant attention — both of which are aimed at Graham
around the clock and around the world. Yet they are also able to
pass along bits and pieces that reflect a pattern of his personality
that can be valued and prized.

Here is a man who sought out Ted Kennedy after he broke his
back in a private plane crash and, without press or publicity, went
to his bedside and asked for God's healing spirit to be in his body
and with his family.

Here is a traveler moving swiftly through an air terminal, with
raincoat collar turned up, dark glasses fixed, and scooping up an
elderly woman's bag, directing her to the ground transportation
— never recognized as Billy Graham, just a smiling middle-aged
man helping a woman out of an airport.

Here is a traveling evangelist, sitting at the breakfast table,
asking about my new parish in Albuquerque, praying publicly
and softly for the food about to be served in the lounge, and then
asking carefully, "Would you pray for me and Ruth?" (Ruth
Graham had been disabled for nearly six months. She had suffered a severe memory loss, having fallen out of a tree in North
Carolina, where she had been literally out on a limb, attaching a
swing for her grandchildren. Billy noted gently, "At least it was a
worthy project.")

And here is a personality who could have become invisible after
Watergate and unknown to Richard Nixon, yet who again and
again has gone to Nixon's San Clemente exile to bring prayer,
support, and strength to a broken family. Graham had shared the
celebrations of the past, and now the inner spirit reveals that he is
prepared to share the shame of the present. In these and many
other vignettes you are given a portrait of why Billy Graham is as
he is.

One day the Christian world will learn of the passing of Billy
Graham. And in that loss his critics within the Church will
discover how great he really was. For there is no other person in
this century, in our time now, who has had the ability to reach so
much of the world with the gospel. And when the summaries are
written and the judgment offered on his life, it will be revealed

that he had become first among Christians, for he had been the servant of all. In the New Testament we read:

> And he sat down and called the twelve; and he said to them, "If any one would be first, he must be last of all and servant of all."
> — Mark 9:35 RSV

PAPER AIRPLANES

Nearly twenty years ago in New York City, three teen-agers piled into a subway car below Grand Central Station. Each, like me, had been given a leaflet urging our attendance at the Graham Crusade starting that night at Madison Square Garden. One youngster promptly expressed his feelings by squashing the sheet into a paper ball and deftly hooking it, basketball-style, into the nearest trash receptacle. His friend, more space oriented, shaped his handbill into a paper glider and launched it the length of the aisle. The third lad read the announcement slowly and then, folding the paper twice, put it into a shirt pocket. Immediately he was elbowed by his friend: "What are you, some kind of saint heading for the Garden?" Laughter. "No," he shrugged, "I just want to see him and hear what he has to say."

In a society that has been nurtured on the antics of the anti-hero and deeply affected by the bravado of the rebel, the renegade, and guerrilla gunfire, it just may be time to hear from a person who offers genuine care and true affection. And it seems to this writer that the staying power of the Southern preacher is to be written in his acts of love and concern, counterbalancing the influence of a treacherous, wretched world.

When the last conclusions about Graham are sifted and recorded, it may be agreed that his greatest gift for the last half of the twentieth century was not that he packed them in at Madison Square or Earls Court or Hollywood Bowl . . . nor the success of radio and television and the soaring accomplishments of publishing. These may amount to naught — and our conclusion would be that lastly Billy Graham had loved people greatly and, by loving them, led them to the gates of the kingdom of God.

And Billy Graham became number one in that he helped countless others to find a Savior, and through the encounter with

Christ, they found their own true fulfillment and service, so that *they*, too, became number one in the kingdom of heaven, servants of all.

Notes

CHAPTER 1

[1]Stanley High, *Billy Graham* (New York: McGraw-Hill, 1956), p. 143.
[2]Billy Graham, *Peace With God* (New York: Doubleday, 1953), p. 14.
[3]Ibid., p. 15.
[4]Ibid., p. 17.
[5]Ibid., pp. 21-22.
[6]Charles Colson, *Born Again* (Old Tappan, N.J.: Fleming H. Revell, Chosen Books, 1976), p. 110.
[7]*Christian Century* 73 (8 August 1956):921.
[8]Ibid.
[9]Ibid., p. 922.
[10]Ibid.
[11]*Time* 66 (21 November 1955).
[12]Ibid.
[13]*Newsweek* 43 (15 March 1954).
[14]Ibid.
[15]Ibid.
[16]*Newsweek* 43 (31 May 1954).
[17]Ibid.
[18]*Christian Century* 71 (24 March 1954).

CHAPTER 2

[1]*U. S. News & World Report* 37 (27 August 1954).

[2]R. B. Robertson, *The Golden Eagle* (New York: Alfred A. Knopf, 1957), pp. 172-73.

[3]*Christian Century* 71 (16 June 1954).

[4]Ibid.

[5]*Saturday Review of Literature* 37 (13 February 1954).

[6]Ibid.

[7]*New Yorker* 31 (25 June 1955).

[8]*Look* 17 (5 May 1953).

[9]Stanley High, *Billy Graham* (New York: McGraw-Hill, 1956), p. 153.

[10]Arthur Lester Frederick, *Christian Century* (23 April 1952):496.

[11]John Pollock, *Crusades: Twenty Years with Billy Graham* (Minneapolis: World Wide Publications, 1969), p. 104.

[12]*New Republic* 133 (22 August 1955).

[13]Myrick Land, *The Fine Art of Literary Mayhem* (New York: Holt, Rinehart & Winston, n.d.).

[14]Somerset Maugham, *Maugham's Choice of Kipling's Best* (New York: Doubleday, 1953).

[15]*Nation* 186 (8 February 1958).

[16]Ross Watson, *Smithsonian* 6 (March 1977):103.

[17]*Christian Century* (15 May 1957).

CHAPTER 3

[1]The *Sunday Telegraph* (London), 9 April 1972: as quoted in Christopher Moody, *Solzhenitsyn* (New York: Harper & Row, 1975), p.84.

[2]Theodore Roszak, *The Making of a Counter-Culture* (New York: Doubleday, 1969), p. 14.

[3]*Christianity Today* 13 (June 1969):35.

[4]Roszak, *Making of a Counter-Culture*, pp. 15-16.

[5-12]*My Answer* by Billy Graham; *Christian Herald* and *Signs of Our Times* (London), 30 August 1969.

CHAPTER 4

[1]Ernie Pyle from David Poling's notes.

[2]Arthur Koestler from David Poling's notes.

[3]*Look* 17 (5 May 1953).

[4]Paul Short in *The Billy Graham Crusade News* in New York (January 1957): p. 2.

CHAPTER 6

[1]John Pollock, *Crusades: Twenty Years with Billy Graham* (Minneapolis: World Wide Publications, 1969), p. 100.

[2]Billy Graham, *The Jesus Generation* (Minneapolis: World Wide Publications, 1971), p. 18.
[3]Ibid., p. 25.
[4]*Christian Century* 77 (17 February 1960).
[5]*Saturday Evening Post* 236 (13 April 1963).
[6]Carl F. H. Henry in *Christianity Today:* from David Poling's notes.

CHAPTER 7

[1]Lewis Gillenson, *Billy Graham and Seven Who Were Saved* (New York: Simon & Schuster, Trident Press, 1967), p. 18.
[2]*U. S. Catholic* 41 (March 1976).
[3]Ibid.
[4]Ibid.
[5]Billy Graham, *Peace With God* (New York: Doubleday, 1953), p. 28.
[6]Billy Graham, *World Aflame* (New York: Doubleday, 1965), p. xv.
[7]Ibid.
[8]George Burnham, *Billy Graham: Mission Accomplished* (Old Tappan, N.J.: Fleming H. Revell, 1955), p. 89.
[9]Stanley High, *Billy Graham* (New York: McGraw-Hill, 1956), p. 241.
[10]*The Billy Graham Crusade News* in New York (January 1957).
[11]Graham, *World Aflame*, p. 183.
[12]Ibid.
[13]Ibid., p. xiii.
[14]Ibid., p. xiv.
[15]Billy Graham, *The Jesus Generation* (Minneapolis: World Wide Publications, 1971), p. 150.
[16]Ibid., p. 61.
[17]Graham, *World Aflame*, p. 56.
[18]Graham, *Peace With God*, p. 131.
[19]Ibid., p. 141.

CHAPTER 8

Sermon: From *Those Who Came Forward* by Curtis Mitchell (Philadelphia: Chilton, 1966).
[1]*Atlantic Monthly* 200 (September 1957).
[2]Ibid.

CHAPTER 9

[1]Theodore Ferris, *The Image of God in Christ* (New York: Oxford University Press, 1965), p. 52.
[2]Ibid., p. 55.
[3]Ibid., p. 56.

[4]*U. S. Catholic* 41 (March 1976).

[5]Gilbert Barnes, *Letters of Theodore Weld* (Gloucester, Mass.: Peter Smith, Publisher, 1934).

[6]E. Stanley Jones, *Christian Century* 74 (August 1970).

[7]Billy Graham, *Decision Magazine* (February 1976).

[8]Ibid.

[9]Ibid.

[10]Ibid.

[11]Edward B. Fiske, "The Closest Thing to a White House Chaplain," *New York Times Magazine* (8 June 1969).

[12]John Corry, *Harper's Magazine* 238 (February 1969).

CHAPTER 10

[1]*Atlantic Monthly* 200 (September 1957).

[2]William G. McLoughlin, *Billy Graham: Revivalist in a Secular Age* (New York: Ronald Press Co., 1960), p. 223.

[3]Ibid., p. 209.

[4]Billy Graham, *Angels: God's Secret Agents* (New York: Doubleday, 1975), p. 5.

[5]Ibid., p. x.

[6]Ibid.

[7]Ibid.

[8]*Christianity Today* 15 (6 November 1970).

[9]*Commonweal* (July 1976).

[10]Graham, *Angels*, p. 73.

[11]John Pollock, *Crusades: Twenty Years with Billy Graham* (Minneapolis: World Wide Publications, 1969), p. 271.